SECRETS OF RESILIENT PEOPLE

50 Techniques You Need to Be Strong

John Lees

This book, like my first, is dedicated to my wife Jan,
for being the best thing.

# SECRETS OF
# RESILIENT PEOPLE

50 Techniques You Need to Be Strong

**John Lees**

First published in Great Britain in 2014 by Hodder and Stoughton. An Hachette UK company.

First published in US in 2014 by The McGraw-Hill Companies, Inc.

This edition published 2014

*British Library Cataloguing in Publication Data*: a catalogue record for this title is available from the British Library.

*Library of Congress Catalog Card Number*: on file.

Paperback ISBN 9781473600218

ebook ISBN 9781473600232

10 9 8 7 6 5 4 3 2 1

Typeset by Cenveo® Publisher Services.

Printed and bound in Great Britain by CPI Group (UK) Ltd., Croydon, CR0 4YY.

John Murray Learning policy is to use papers that are natural, renewable and recyclable products and made from wood grown in sustainable forests. The logging and manufacturing processes are expected to conform to the environmental regulations of the country of origin.

John Murray Learning

338 Euston Road

London NW1 3BH

www.hodder.co.uk

# CONTENTS

This SECRETS book contains a number of special textual features, which have been developed to help you navigate the chapters quickly and easily. Throughout the book, you will find these indicated by the following icons.

 Each chapter contains quotes from inspiring figures. These will be useful for helping you understand different viewpoints and why each secret is useful in a practical context.

 Also included in each chapter are a number of strategies that outline techniques for putting this secret into practice.

 The putting it all together box at the end of each chapter provides a summary of each chapter, and a quick way into the core concepts of each secret.

12
13
(14)
15

You'll also see a chapter ribbon down the right hand side of each right-hand page, to help you mark your progress through the book and to make it easy to refer back to a particular chapter you found useful or inspiring.

# INTRODUCTION

## What is resilience?

> '*I am sure it is everyone's experience, as it has been mine, that any discovery we make about ourselves or the meaning of life is never, like a scientific discovery, a coming upon something entirely new and unsuspected; it is rather, the coming to conscious recognition of something, which we really knew all the time but, because we were unwilling to formulate it correctly, we did not hitherto know we knew.*' W. H. Auden, Markings

Human beings respond in different ways to external forces. Even a minor knock-back can weaken self-esteem in some people with a measurable impact on their work performance. Others weather storms with little or no effect on their efficiency or sense of well-being. Some crumble, some cope, some not only survive but thrive under considerable pressure. This is resilience. We want to know what drives it, why some people lack it, and whether it can be strengthened.

In physics the term 'resilience' describes a quality in a material which influences the speed at which it will return to its former shape after being bent, compressed or stressed. This quality is associated with elasticity and response to stress. It's useful to remember this baseline definition, because when we consider resilience in people we usually think of stress in negative terms. However in the physical world stress can be useful, for example in a spring or cantilever bridge. Some external stresses in human experience are equally productive – a pressing deadline being one obvious example.

In their book **Resilience: Why Things Bounce Back** (Business Plus, 2012) Andrew Zolli and Ann Marie Healy offer this comprehensive definition: 'the capacity of a system, enterprise, or a person to maintain its core purpose and integrity in the face of dramatically changed circumstances'. The phrase 'core purpose and integrity' hints that resilience is about more than survival or coping; it might be about growth towards a healthier equilibrium.

Human resilience is the ability to bounce back; in business terms, the ability to resume normal service delivery after a crisis. Sometimes this relates to the short term; getting your 'mojo' back after a disappointment or rejection. At other times the process is one of re-discovering self-esteem and sense of purpose at a deeper level. It's about the way we deal with all threats to well-being and continuity – life's road bumps. Some are possible but not certain (loss of role and status through redundancy, for example), while others (ageing, declining health, bereavement) are fairly inevitable.

Resilience is not the same as tough-mindedness, but they are closely related. Tough-mindedness encompasses other qualities such as determination and being strong-willed, and sometimes means avoiding seeing things through other people's eyes. Resilience, on the other hand, can be found in the quietest as well as the brashest people.

## How the idea has taken hold

*'Resilience: the capacity of an individual, community or system to adapt in order to sustain an acceptable level of function, structure, and identity'.* Cabinet Office, March 2011

Psychologists have been interested in resilience for over half a century. Early studies followed the lives of children who became refugees because of the Second World War, including Holocaust survivors. Psychologists were puzzled why some children quickly adjusted to balanced, purposeful lives, and others – including siblings – had debilitating problems even as adults. Early work therefore had a big focus on child development, but went on to look at the way adults respond to life-disrupting episodes or events.

More recently resilience has focused on those who go to war. Studies have asked why some military personnel suffer long-term post-traumatic stress disorder (PTSD) while others with similarly grim experiences suffer few effects, or none at all.

Resilience is a term measuring the capacity of communities to rebuild themselves after natural catastrophes, some involving extreme deprivation and starvation, and how quickly services can be restored. The term is also used to describe how communities redefine themselves following downturns including the disappearance of traditional industries.

Resilience is not just about metals and people. In ecology, resilience describes the ability of an ecosystem to survive damage or pollution. In the business world resilient systems have multiple levels of backup in place to prevent loss of service in an emergency. The US Agency for International Development defines resilience as 'the ability of people, households, communities, countries, and systems to mitigate, adapt to and recover from shocks and stresses in a manner that reduces chronic vulnerability and facilitates inclusive growth'.

## Why are we so interested in resilience?

66 *'The great surprise of resilience research is the ordinariness of the phenomena. Resilience appears to be an ordinary phenomenon that results in most cases from the operation of basic human adaptational systems.'* Ann Masten

Why is resilience such a hot topic in the early twenty-first century? Various explanations offer themselves.

Firstly, our awareness of natural disasters has increased. Whether they are happening more often is unclear, but when they occur we feel present because eyewitness interviews and video footage are broadcast within minutes. When tsunamis, earthquakes and forest fires burst onto screens instantly we naturally imagine what it must be like to go through the experience. Part of us wonders how we would react, and how long it would take to return to normal. Studies of resilience look at communities recovering from such events, such as the Japanese tsunami of 2012 which killed nearly 16,000 people. We're interested in how communities re-invent themselves after massive disruption, and why some succeed brilliantly.

Resilience is also important to ordinary working lives. It's required because of the relentless acceleration of change in our society. In an age of information overload our days are spent running faster just to catch up. The economic downturn means that redundancy is a common experience across sectors.

Organizations are merged, acquired or restructured at lightning speed. Workers frequently find themselves undertaking the work of two or more people, and have become used to the fact that every year or two they may have to apply for their own jobs. Many hold down more than one paid job; others live with the uncertainty of zero-hours contracts. The recession has not only tested resilience, but placed it centre stage as an important tool in every worker's survival kit.

We might set Western society's preoccupation with resilience in a global context. You may be reeling from a negative appraisal, or the news that your job is under threat – such events can have a huge emotional impact. Yet it's easy to forget that on an international scale these are modest tests of resilience. You might be worrying about a business presentation or appraisal, but much of the world's population worries about finding clean water. You might be worried about falling income, but it's unlikely that you will be forced into the toxic and dangerous work currently undertaken by workers in the world's nastiest unregulated industries. In comparison most of our work problems are pretty small, and soon past.

## Where does it come from?

Are you born resilient, or do you learn it? Some people seem to have resilience in their genes. Military psychologists dealing with PTSD look for a base level of resistance to unpleasant events, finding that some people are more prone to anxiety, hyperattentiveness and other states triggered by high-stress events, while others experience few long-term effects. It appears that some of us have a natural ability to resume our former mental 'shape' almost without interruption, for example in the face of grief or separation, while others spend the rest of their lives trying to rediscover lost confidence and peace of mind.

Psychologist Abraham Maslow saw what he termed a 'continental divide' between those who start life vulnerable to external pressure, and those who are likely to bounce back: 'stress will break people altogether if they are in the beginning too weak to stand distress, or else, if they are already strong enough to take the stress in the first place, that same stress, if they come through it, will strengthen them, temper them, and make them stronger.'

If some resilience is hard-wired from birth, the remainder is very clearly influenced by our environment. The first major influence is upbringing (a happy childhood and loving parents are identified as important factors). The second is having supportive people close by (strong friendships, a good social network, and feeling part of a community all assist). Studies have examined the way people who have felt low and purposeless for many years can achieve surprising breakthroughs, usually through encounters with other people. These factors help us develop what child psychologist Emmy Werner described as 'reserve capacity' – the buffer we are able to place between ourselves and adverse circumstances. Resilience helps not just with mind state, but also with physical health and speed of recovery from illness. For example, Mary Steinhardt at the University of Texas at Austin has shown that African American adults with type 2 diabetes were helped by resilience-building exercises to self-manage their disease more successfully.

Resilience is rather like patience. Some are born with it, others learn to behave patiently, but a small number grow through self-awareness to be patient people. Our resilience seems to change depending on what is thrown at us, and what resources we can draw upon to help. So you might be more resilient if given time to deal with issues, especially if you have support while you do so and some protection from the next round of disruption. In simple terms, a bit of TLC and a few months where life is a bit quieter can do a power of good.

Therefore the ability to recover comes not just from inner strengths but also outside resources, many of which are within your control. For example, you can choose to find people who are supporters: soul friends, coaches, mentors. You can learn to monitor, check and distract yourself from negative thinking. You might learn how to solve problems and make better decisions more effectively, or to reframe your picture of the world.

## How learning about resilience helps

‘The world breaks everyone, and afterward, some are strong at the broken places.’ Ernest Hemingway

This book is written in the belief that human beings can adapt, learn and grow. Positive psychology offers a fresh approach to any sense that we 'work through' negative thoughts and 'deal with' downbeat experiences: new approaches elevate the importance of simple acts of gratitude and of remembering uplifting events. Relatively small adjustments to mindset can have a major impact on well-being and optimism. This is what Ann Masten famously described in **American Psychologist** (the official journal of the American Psychological Association) as 'ordinary magic'; 'positive adaptation to adversity despite serious threats to adaptation or development'.

Yes, resilience comes more naturally to some, but the good news is that those of us who are not born robust can work in the right direction. Resilience isn't a quality, but an approach, a way of putting your brain in a different gear. It's not a trait, but a process.

Managing your resilience isn't a quick fix. Like all important personal development it requires commitment to the long game. It involves work. The work requires you to adjust habits and consciously adopt new ways of thinking, and then try out new behaviours.

Resilience can be learned, developed, and strengthened; you can teach it to others. You can identify and guard the things that protect it for you. These factors building your 'reserve capacity' are not accidental; they can be negotiated. You can learn to see yourself as others see you, and to improve your organizational fit and contribution. You can find people who will challenge but also affirm you. You can learn to go with the grain and improve your working day, or repeatedly place yourself into work environments which drag you down. You can choose to take more care of your health, and take more time for the things that matter. You can learn to play the hand you've been dealt rather than endlessly wishing for a new deal.

The tips and strategies in this book will provide you with a direction of travel and a few tools for the journey. Informed by good business and coaching sense, these chapters are designed to add a few hardening layers of resilient varnish. If there are things that can make a difference quickly, this book makes them clear, as well as practical measures to help you avoid problems, and tackle those you can't.

Recognize how much resilience matters to your well-being. If you learn to be a little more resistant, you learn to be more useful to yourself and others. The work involves self-examination, but in moderation, because getting locked in your own thoughts is part of the problem. As a first step, drop the idea that you're struggling alone; recognizing that many others share your insecurities guarantees that you don't become too self-focused. The healthiest resilience often comes from not taking yourself too seriously.

# Check your resilience levels

*'The most resilient people are like children who never grew up. A curious, playful spirit contributes directly to resiliency because playfulness and asking questions let you learn your way out of difficult circumstances.'* Al Siebert

*'Happiness is an attitude. We either make ourselves miserable, or happy and strong. The amount of work is the same.'*
Francesca Reigler

*'Success consists of going from failure to failure without loss of enthusiasm.'* Winston Churchill

*'I don't like people who have never fallen or stumbled. Their virtue is lifeless and it isn't of much value. Life hasn't revealed its beauty to them.'* Boris Pasternak

*'One can choose to go back toward safety or forward toward growth. Growth must be chosen again and again; fear must be overcome again and again.'* Abraham Maslow

You can't change your entire personality. What you can do is to understand yourself better, and adjust how you act.

Becoming more aware of how your brain is hard-wired will explain why some relationships don't work and why you operate better in some environments. For example, learning you're someone who needs regular feedback and encouragement means you can exercise more care when choosing contexts, or you can compensate (for example by working with a mentor).

The second step is starting to change behaviours. If your learning style means you work best with explicit instructions, get better at asking for them without sounding incompetent or lacking in resources. Draw on other people's strengths; enlisting a 'people person' to help you pitch a difficult idea to a team meeting covers your blind side (see Chapter 40 on decoding people to cover your gaps in people situations).

This book explores resilience by investigating many ways in which new insights and behaviours can help you adapt, grow, survive with more integrity intact, and sometimes flourish. We begin by checking your current state. In the three tables below give yourself a score using the five-point scale.

If you are unsure what to score, put down your best estimate and a question mark. In the last column tick any factors that are very important to you right now; double tick any that are vitally important.

## MONITORING YOUR BASE-LINE PERSONAL RESILIENCE

High = 5, Uncertain = 3, Low = 1

| Resilience factor | Score | Tick |
|---|---|---|
| How far do you feel you have control over the major events shaping your life? | | |
| How far do you believe in your own capabilities and strengths? | | |
| How far do you feel you have the personal resources to make positive changes happen? | | |
| How far do you feel that important aspects of your future are within your control? | | |
| How confident are you in your ability to acquire new skills and knowledge? | | |
| How optimistic are you generally? | | |
| How optimistic are you even in when things are difficult? | | |
| How good are you at not allocating blame when things start to go wrong? | | |

| Resilience factor | Score | Tick |
|---|---|---|
| How good are you at not blaming yourself as soon as things begin to go wrong? | | |
| How good are you at looking at facts rather than getting emotionally involved in events? | | |
| How much are you aware of your emotional responses to events? | | |
| How much are you aware of the way your emotions impact on others? | | |
| How strong is your self-esteem most of the time? | | |
| How good are you at recognizing your feelings and understanding what triggers them? | | |
| How far do you feel you have grown as a result of life events? | | |
| How good are you at finding humour in a stressful situation? | | |
| How far are you able to remain calm when under moderate pressure? | | |
| How good are you at making difficult decisions? | | |
| How easy do you find it to modify your behaviours when you face repeated problems? | | |
| How successful are you in avoiding worry or anxiety? | | |
| How strong is your ability to persevere with a task when things aren't going well? | | |
| How successful are you in maintaining a healthy lifestyle? | | |
| How successful are you in moderating your intake of sugar, caffeine and alcohol and other substances with negative effects? | | |
| How successful are you in getting enough rest and sleep? | | |
| Other personal factors that matter to you: | | |

# MONITORING YOUR RESILIENCE AT WORK

High = 5, Uncertain = 3, Low = 1

| Resilience factor | Score | Tick |
|---|---|---|
| How far do you feel your work is meaningful or purposeful? | | |
| How far do you feel your work history has met your expectations? | | |
| How strongly would you agree with the statement that you are in control of your career? | | |
| How far do you feel your contribution makes a difference? | | |
| How much of your working life allows you to continue learning? | | |
| How far do you feel valued at work? | | |
| How good are you at motivating yourself? | | |
| How good is your ability to solve problems under pressure? | | |
| How good are you at coping with repeated change? | | |
| How adaptable are you when the rules of the game change rapidly? | | |
| How well trained and skilled do you feel for the work you do? | | |
| How positive do you feel about your work colleagues? | | |
| How far are you able to keep learning in your current role? | | |

| Resilience factor | Score | Tick |
|---|---|---|
| How confident do you feel about your ability to accomplish your career goals? | | |
| How secure do you feel in work? | | |
| How strong are your relationships with senior staff at work who make decisions about your future? | | |
| How far do you experience autonomy at work? (Feeling that you have control over decisions, and how and when you perform tasks). | | |
| How well do you cope with conflict? | | |
| How good are you at getting on with your work after experiencing rejection or personal criticism? | | |
| How far do your emotions impact on your work performance? | | |
| How strong is the network of people whom you really trust? | | |
| How far are you supported by a mentor? | | |
| What is the level of encouragement you receive from work colleagues? | | |
| How easy is it for you to switch off after your working day? | | |
| Other work-related factors that matter to you: | | |

# MONITORING RESILIENCE-SHAPING RELATIONSHIPS

High = 5, Uncertain = 3, Low = 1

| Resilience factor | Score | Tick |
|---|---|---|
| How much do you rely on others to help you cope with daily adversity? | | |
| How strong are your close personal relationships, including friendships? | | |
| How strongly would you agree with the statement 'I have several people around me who listen to me without judging me and give me unconditional support'? | | |
| How strongly would you agree with the statement 'I trust my colleagues'? | | |
| How strongly would you agree with the statement 'I am trusted by my colleagues'? | | |
| How easy is it for you to talk about strong feelings? | | |
| How easy is it for you to be honest about disappointment? | | |
| How strong are your confiding relationships, where you tell someone how you are really feeling? | | |
| How far do you feel your opinions are heard and valued by others? | | |
| How good are you at resisting manipulation or flattery? | | |
| How much do you rely on regular praise to keep your spirits up? | | |
| How effective are you at saying 'no' to work which you can't manage without making mistakes? | | |
| How good are you at coping with rejection? | | |

6

| Resilience factor | Score | Tick |
|---|---|---|
| How easy do you find it to work in a team where you are given little feedback about how you are doing? | | |
| How easy do you find it to describe any sense of vulnerability or isolation you may feel? | | |
| How would you describe the levels of emotional support available to you from other people? | | |
| How strongly are you connected to the community where you live? | | |
| How active are you in sports or hobbies that require you to engage with others? | | |
| How far are your personal values expressed in out of work activities, for example helping a charity or being part of a community of faith? | | |
| Other relationship-related factors that matter to you: | | |

### Putting it all together

These questionnaires provide no overall scores, nor is there any kind of simplistic reference to the 'average'. Your scores are entirely subjective, and that's deliberate. The most important result is the range of conversations you can have drawing upon this material; discussing it with a friend or coach may provide important insights into areas where your resilience is challenged, or will be in the future. Talk about your scores and why you gave them, but also the factors you have ticked as important to you right now.

Look first of all at areas in which you have scored a 1 or 2. These are areas of risk and vulnerability. These topics should give you useful prompts about which tips in this book to read first. These scores may reveal that you're operating way outside your comfort zone (perhaps in a high-stress environment, or one where you get no feedback).

Factors where you have scored 3 also need your attention, but not quite so urgently.

Now consider factors where you have scored 4 or 5. These are areas where your resilience appears to have protection at the moment. This may come from innate characteristics, experience, or the circumstances you find yourself in now. Don't take these areas of strength for granted. Protect them where appropriate, and build on them.

# 2 Fail forwards, not backwards

**❝** *'I have not failed. I've just found 10,000 ways that won't work.'*
Thomas Edison

**❝** *'Success has many fathers, but failure is an orphan.'*
Unknown origin, probably an Italian proverb

**❝** *'Learn from the mistakes of others. You can never live long enough to make them all yourself.'* Groucho Marx

**❝** *'Mistakes are the portals of discovery.'* James Joyce

**❝** *'People often ask me, "Do you ever give advice to young actors?" I say no. Never. And they say, "Why not?" And I say, "Because the only advice I ever got from more experienced older actors was to give it up." They all looked at me and said, "Give it up Michael, you're not going to make it." Every single person said the same thing: give it up. But I have some sort of built in insanity so I never stopped. I didn't give it up.'* Michael Caine

What is failure? To some, a vital learning experience. Many millionaires have several failed businesses in their past. 'Failing forward' is about thinking differently about these experiences. You can choose to dwell in regret, beat yourself up about past decisions – or you can focus your failure 'forwards' to prevent repetition rather than remaining stuck in the past. Failing forward is about learning enough and then moving on.

Alastair Campbell, reflecting on his time advising Tony Blair, famously said that in politics people move overnight 'from hero to zero' in the public's perception. In a world of information overload we need to process quickly; black and white is easier to think about than grey. Perfection is the new standard. While some maturely strive to be 'good enough' partners, parents, co-workers or managers, many feel under tremendous daily pressure to achieve 100% every time. This forces us to adopt 'either/or' thinking – if it's not a success, it must be a failure.

Self-criticism can easily tip into hard absolutes, so we measure too many things in terms of total success or abject failure. We're conditioned to list successes only and to hide failures in interviews or appraisals. This goes against the grain of the way human beings learn; we don't improve by patting ourselves on the back for perfection every day, but by making mistakes. To allow yourself to make mistakes requires a degree of risk, uncertainty and vulnerability.

This easily spills over into the way we talk about ourselves. Since we are highly attuned to negative information and the media prefers bad news to good, we are far more likely to remember stories of failure, which means that the way we describe our low points shapes our reputation.

The concept of 'fail forwards' is helpful because it encourages just enough reflection to allow us to move on to the next stage. Yes, review what went well and what didn't. Look objectively at the things you could have done better, but don't get locked into your reflective process. The past is educational, but it's too easy to get stuck there.

## AVOID LOOKING BACK FOR TOO LONG

Learning resilience requires you to challenge what you think of as your failures, and not to give them more of your attention than they deserve.

This is not permission for you to gloss over or ignore those moments when you really should have said or done something different. Rethinking failure is about recognizing the point where healthy reflection tips into beating yourself up. Spot where reflection becomes recrimination. Looking back is fine for short periods, but 'failing forwards' is about beginning the next project, starting the next day.

Do review, but only once, and not for too long. Set time aside to look at a situation or event, ideally alongside someone who witnessed what happened. Write down up to three things you would do differently if the situation came up again. That's it. Three things. If the list is any longer you won't do anything about it, and you'll keep adding to it. If you need coaching, training or a pep talk to help you do those things, arrange that now.

Look at the next time you are unsuccessful pitching a proposal at work. Ignore feelings of recrimination – yes, of course you could have prepared better, but that's nearly always the case even when you're successful. Take a minute to jot down why you didn't achieve your aim, what can improve and what approach you'll try next time. Then move on.

## FOCUS ON WHAT YOU CAN CHANGE

Try to review past actions differently with a focus always on failing forwards. Do this by reviewing events only in the light of the things you can change. So, for example, if a meeting didn't go well and you rubbed somebody up the wrong way, there are plenty of things you can do about that. You can be honest about your sense that the meeting didn't go too well.

Failing backwards means that you obsess about your past choices and actions. It's hard to be objective when you do that, and even if you are there comes a point when you should switch your focus from then to now.

Apologize, but don't over-do it. Apologizing is an important way to show empathy and responsibility, but always apologizing for everything can make you seem weak (see Chapter 8). So if you and a colleague have very different perceptions of a decision made at a meeting, it does no harm to say 'Sorry, I seem to have misunderstood'. As long as you don't take it too literally, or take it to heart. Human beings can misread each other or situations perfectly easily without any help from you. Things get missed, wires get crossed. The real question is whether you forgot to do something, and can you act differently next time? If the answer is 'no' to both questions, move on: put your focus on the next step, not the apology.

## TRY STUFF OUT

Adopt the habit of being experimental. To think 'it's all experimental' is a great approach to life. If you don't experiment, you don't discover. You will know that every great discovery or invention came on the back of repeated so-called failures. The light bulb was only invented after dozens of alternative designs failed.

Experimenting is sometimes about thinking creatively, but always about having an open mind. Don't pre-judge, don't decide what will work and what won't. Take appropriate risks with your work experiments, and welcome false starts and failures as evidence which helps you along the way.

Value mistakes (including those others make) if they teach you something worth knowing. Avoid negative thinking when experiments go wrong. Experiment and failure, 'making mistakes', is a necessary part of creative thinking. It's a well-known fact that behind every new business idea there's a long list of things that didn't quite come off. Before every new invention comes a history of failed attempts. You can't make progress without getting things wrong some of the time. If you are going to focus on failure, then draw on it as a learning experience, but don't let road bumps spoil the journey. Every successful product brought to market required a thousand near-misses. Experiment away.

### Putting it all together

Some people make mistakes without noticing. They are often the most difficult colleagues because they have major blind spots about their performance and their impact on others. Some people make errors of judgement but refuse to learn from them, refusing to see the problem or blaming someone else.

If you're a person who naturally reflects on what you do, you may find yourself reviewing the past over and over again, spending a great deal of energy on events or encounters that are long gone. Beating yourself up for past actions can become self-indulgent, and doing it too much takes you beyond learning from mistakes and into fear of failure. This shifts your instincts to risk avoidance. Letting things go is a good way of switching energy from past experience to future possibilities.

Resilient learners incorporate negative as well as positive results into their approach to life. They know when to risk through experiment, and have learned not to be discouraged when things don't work.

Failing forwards is about building on even the harshest setbacks and coming out the other side with new creativity, spiced with a little wisdom. It's a healthy mindset for dealing with mistakes, near-misses and occasional disasters. It reveals the point when reflection becomes indulgent recrimination. It isn't about sweeping things under the carpet or pretending that problems don't exist. It's about honestly looking at mistakes so you learn and do something new. Learn from the past but don't live in it.

# 3 Look at what's working, not what isn't

> **66** 'We do not deal much in facts when we are contemplating ourselves.' Mark Twain

> **66** 'Failure is the condiment that gives success its flavour.' Truman Capote

> **66** 'Don't confuse me with facts, my mind is made up.' Unknown origin

> **66** 'To be interested in the changing seasons is a happier state of mind than to be hopelessly in love with spring.' George Santayana

> **66** 'Man, they said we better accentuate the positive
> Eliminate the negative
> Latch on to the affirmative
> Don't mess with Mister In-Between.' Johnny Mercer, 1944

Trainee airline pilots are taught, in an emergency, not to focus on what has failed, but to make a quick assessment of systems that are still functioning: What do I have left working which will get me safely on the ground? This vital training provokes an immediate switch from past (what has already happened) to future (what can happen next), reinforcing the fact that this is not a moment for analysis or recrimination. Very importantly this thinking also takes the focus away from what has already failed in order to put complete attention on what hasn't: all the resources available to get a planeload of passengers onto the tarmac.

Under pressure it's easy to put all your focus on what isn't working. Pilot training shows us that we can learn to switch focus, quickly, on to the things that will enable us to rescue a situation. It's all about where your attention rests. You can choose to commit all your energy to the problem, listing everything that's going wrong. This is rarely about facts, and very often really means 'look at how badly life is treating me'. Through frustration that the game isn't playing out right for you, your attention is seduced into feeling victimized (see Chapter 6).

If things are going wrong, sometimes it's chance, sometimes there's a reason. However, while things are going wrong the difference doesn't matter; that's a luxury that will have to wait until you have time to review. Right now you can choose where to direct your energy – yourself, or the problem.

Make a choice. Choose to focus on those things which are still working, the things remaining in your toolkit which can save the day. If the system has gone down, what can be done manually? If a key person has fallen ill, who can step in quickly? What's the most important thing to be fixed first?

It's easy to spend all your time and energy focusing on conversations that haven't worked, applications that fell at the first hurdle, or people who won't return your call.

## DON'T LET PANIC DIRECT YOUR BEHAVIOURS

Sure, panic is understandable. The problem is that panic has two dimensions – one is sudden anxiety, the other is unthinking behaviour. Be careful what buttons you press, what phone number you dial, what files you delete …

The origins of the word 'panic' relate to the Greek god Pan, who regularly scared flocks of animals. It describes the effects of mindless terror: flight rather than fight, doing anything to get away from the suspected source of danger. In work terms this might be a sudden urge to go home early, but usually panic results in the wrong kind of solution. We press the nearest button. We ask for help from people who should be seeing us as independent thinkers. We tell the wrong people about the problem and make them panic too. We overstate the problem, usually declaring total failure: 'it's all gone wrong'.

The command 'don't panic!' sounds nonsensical or unrealistic, a bit like saying 'don't react'. What you can do, however, is take a breath before you do anything as a result of your feelings. Resilience is often about taking a few microseconds between impulse and action. The good news is that this is a discipline you can learn. For a few minutes at least, don't do something, just sit there.

Resilient people learn to put a clear dividing line in their heads between reaction and action. 'This is what's happening' means gathering facts (see Chapter 4), not just registering your own emotions. 'This is how I feel about it' is healthy self-monitoring. Be careful who you share that initial response with; superiors may write off one incident as evidence that you don't manage well in a crisis. Watch your hand as it reaches for a phone, the 'send' button on an email or as it goes into the air to ask for help. Is this immediate impulse right, or are you simply being chased over a cliff liked a panicked sheep?

## DON'T GET DRAWN INTO THE BLAME GAME

It's easy to get bogged down in recriminations. Asking the question 'who is responsible?' is often a way of saying 'don't blame me'. Blame is irrelevant. Even if one person is blatantly at fault, that fact is irrelevant in this moment. Blame is entering an emotional dimension of fault and guilt; it doesn't help you solve the problem.

Equally, don't be tempted to over-analyse things. This doesn't mean forging on blindly without checking the basics (yes, do check if the equipment has been unplugged by accident) or seeing if some obvious error can be resolved. In most situations this deserves three or four minutes of your attention. Any analysis beyond that is about understanding underlying reasons, the cause and effect of what went wrong. That's best done offline, with a calm mind. Saying 'nobody move until we find out why this has gone wrong' simply enforces paralysis.

Don't apply standards of perfection to a quick fix. When, later, you look at system faults and the reasons for equipment failure, or you discover communication problems that led to the error, that's useful information to make long-term improvements. Your immediate solution doesn't need to be elegant as long as it works well enough, whether that means an apologetic phone call or duct tape.

## LOOK AWAY FROM THE PROBLEM, AND CATALOGUE YOUR RESOURCES

Take a breath. Don't let your attention be drawn in to what is broken or failing. Focus on fixing the important things that need solving right now with the resources you have got.

Imagine you're that airline pilot mentioned above, and one engine has just blown out. Look away from that engine. Imagine the dials and switches which show fully functional equipment and systems. Look at the things that are still ticking away, functioning perfectly. Build on what you have available to you.

Identify the problem, then pause. Collect information about what is still working. If it's a technology failure, which parts of the system are still working? What can be fixed quickly, or at least patched up? If someone has let you down, who else is available? Prioritize. What problems can wait until resources come on line?

### Putting it all together

The phrase 'nothing is going right' is nearly always a gross overstatement. It's seeing one incident as the sign of a catastrophe (see Chapter 42) or as part of a malign pattern. It's on the edge of victim mode (see Chapter 6), because you believe the universe is treating you badly.

Bouncing back can be about rejecting that kind of statement from the outset. Something will still be working; it's your job to spot everything that is still capable of nailing the problem. Focusing on what's working means that you have to take your attention away from what is going wrong. Pause as soon as you see the first signs of panic. If you're using a computer, avoid the temptation to press the first button on screen which seems to offer an escape route.

The immediate benefit of seeing the glass half full is that you begin to take yourself out of the picture. Even if you've made a huge mistake, that only matters later. Getting drawn into panic simply means that instinct takes over. However this isn't a creative instinct but the part of your primeval brain that says 'trouble: get me out of here'. Avoidance and guilt are strongly linked, and set your mind gyrating in circles of self-criticism.

Focusing on the things that can rescue a situation means you're more likely to fix the problem on your own. The solution may not win a design award, but a prompt and positive decision is the best decision available.

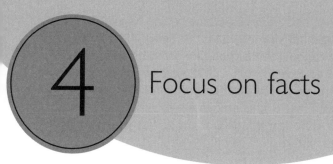

# 4 Focus on facts

**CC** *'Everyone is entitled to his own opinion, but not his own facts.'*
Daniel Patrick Moynihan

**CC** *'Facts do not cease to exist because they are ignored.'*
Aldous Huxley

**CC** *'Mistakes can be corrected by those who pay attention to facts but dogmatism will not be corrected by those who are wedded to a vision.'* Thomas Sowell

**CC** *'Let me dispel a few rumours so they don't fester into facts.'*
Tom Schulman

**CC** *'Exaggeration is truth that has lost its temper.'* Khalil Gibran

When things start to go wrong it often feels like everything has gone wrong. A customer rings up to say that he made an online order six days ago and hasn't heard a thing. Your initial enquiries suggest that you've taken his money but there is no other record of the customer on the system. A colleague suggests that this could have happened hundreds of times this week and no one would have known. Your boss is already making an angry call to the web management team. Two different people have already contacted the customer to apologize, but no one is sure what solution has actually been agreed. Now your team leader wants to check all incoming enquiries and orders this month.

It's all too easy to get caught up in a situation like this. Everything's going wrong. The system is broken. The sky is about to fall in.

It's probably an isolated problem: one person having a bad day, missing a single but vital instruction or detail. The point is that you just don't know yet. Reactions are based on fear, contempt for the work of others, mistrust of IT systems, some vague sense that things are going wrong under the bonnet that you can't see, combined with that mild apprehension experienced by most busy people – the fear that in working so fast you might have made a huge mistake.

Situations like this kick up a cloud of emotional dust, but the calm mind begins by pinning down facts. Even when the office is going to hell in a handcart, it always helps if someone asks what, exactly has happened. When a few things go wrong it's easy to generalize, seeing chaos and catastrophe (see Chapter 42), and that makes it hard to begin to solve problems. Instead, isolate the issue and work out what aspect of it needs urgent attention.

The resilient mind looks for the best route to safe ground, not the quickest. Beware of jumping at a quick fix based on second-hand information, or arriving at the most obvious conclusion because of emotional coercion.

## SEPARATE FACTS FROM NOISE

At the beginning of a long train journey I discovered that my phone wouldn't send emails or texts. Instead of getting on with other work, I started turning things on and off, re-installing passwords, rebooting, reformatting – activities which took about one and a half hours of tinkering.

I was listening to noise, not facts. Noise is what rushes in as soon as something goes wrong. The noise became a conclusion: 'I've altered my phone settings by mistake', reinforced by a desire to fix things. A better response would have been to leave my phone alone for 30 minutes. A quick online search that evening confirmed that the whole network had crashed that day.

The problem with noise is that it is more intriguing and more pressing than mere facts. If your car dies suddenly it's more exciting to run a movie in your head about engine failure or the death of your electronics. It could be that you ignored the fuel warning.

People who work in high-pressure environments are taught
to check facts before making assumptions. This often requires
the discipline of boring, systematic fault checking. Is it switched
on at the plug? Have you changed any of the settings? Did the
envelope go in the post or is it still in your briefcase?

The danger is seeing things the way they should be, rather than
how they are. That's why people leave their car keys on the
hallstand, because their brain tells them the keys are in their
pocket. You may think you've looked everywhere, but perhaps
you haven't started looking properly at all.

## DON'T BELIEVE PANIC STATEMENTS

Remember when you lost something vital in your home,
saying 'I've looked for it everywhere!', followed by copious bad
language? You've probably ruled out places because they are
unlikely. The reason that a calm person can find something is that
they have fewer preconceptions about where not to look, and
they are less likely to look without seeing.

The same thing applies to information supplied under pressure.
The reason the patient young man on the IT helpline asks
you the question 'is your printer connected to a power supply?'
is that under stress we are blind to the obvious and see what
we expect to see. So a missing file may be in plain sight, and keys
may in fact be in the key drawer.

When people supply you with information in a hurry they make
mistakes. You may begin a witch-hunt into the reasons your
customer didn't receive a vital parcel. Before you start blaming IT,
the post room or the mailman, it's worth checking whether the
order was ever submitted.

Believing that facts are absolute leads to rule statements. 'I've
looked everywhere' isn't a statement of fact, but an expression
of frustration. 'We didn't get the order out' may be a fact,
but could equally be emotional noise, an unwarranted dark
thought: the item could be sitting, safely delivered, in the client's
reception area.

# MISTRUST SECOND-HAND INFORMATION

When someone is describing a crisis or emergency, look hard for facts, and look even harder at the emotional filters applied by others. A neighbour rings your doorbell and tells you 'dial 999 – there's been a terrible accident!'. This could involve several people and vehicles, or one cat. This information is second-hand. All you know is that something has happened that this witness feels is terrible and thinks is an accident.

Check second-hand information carefully, and diplomatically. The question 'are you sure?' is pretty insulting. Encourage people to talk you through the facts. Let them tell the whole thing quickly, and then get them to talk it through slowly while you ask fact-based questions like 'what exactly did he say?' and 'how do you know that?'.

Be open to the possibility that you may be part of the problem. It may be you saying 'our website is down' when one enquirer can't log on. Check your own absolute statements. If you're caught up in the situation emotionally because you're worried or angry, run the facts by someone who you know is a calm, cautious thinker before you charge in shouting 'fire' (and see Chapter 42 on Chicken Little Syndrome).

### Putting it all together

In heated situations, hunches, guesses and rash opinion are easy to find. Statements about where the finger should be pointed are often simply expressions of frustration. We see patterns and conspiracies: one thing may have gone awry, but to the jaundiced mind unrelated errors look like a sequence. Gather in facts patiently. Listen to stories twice: once so you can separate emotional content from facts, the second time for important details. Resist the temptation to know why before you learn about what, when and how.

Collect hard facts, and keep asking questions. Facts are easily distorted in the heat of the moment; emotional responses make them easy to suppress or push out. Slowing things down to establish a history gives clarity to decision-making, even if you have to postpone discovering why something went wrong. Grasping at solutions before you have cold evidence usually adds to the problem.

In any crisis it's healthy to think forward – running a movie in your head imagining the time when things will be under control. Picturing that end point leads to a calmer approach, simply because you're recognizing that most problems have some kind of solution.

Learn to mistrust, and possibly ignore, the wrapper that rushed information arrives in, especially when it's set out in hard and fast rules. Issues that appear black and white often respond best to grey solutions. It's a sound strategy to mistrust all absolute statements until they have been tested at least once.

# 5 Reframe your experience

❝ 'Whether you think you can or you think you can't, you're right.'
Henry Ford

❝ 'We choose our joys and sorrows long before we experience them.' Khalil Gibran

❝ 'If you don't like something, change it; if you can't change it, change the way you think about it.' Mary Engelbreit

❝ 'The pessimist complains about the wind; the optimist expects it to change; the realist adjusts the sails.' William Arthur Ward

❝ 'Attitude is a little thing that makes a big difference.'
Winston Churchill

Before CCTV cameras, the police relied on eyewitnesses. Magistrates knew that where there were multiple witnesses there were multiple perspectives. This doesn't mean that each witness sees things entirely differently, but important details will often change. Those taking witness statements know that it's more important to check facts (see Chapter 4) than to gain impressions; the phrase 'the car raced down the street' doesn't mean anything objectively.

We don't record our lives like a bank of video cameras. We edit, interpret, and add information that seems to fit. In work terms, although there is often a broad consensus ('the conference went pretty well'), individual perceptions vary. This isn't just about viewpoint – where you were sitting, what you could see and hear – it's also about attitude. If you started a conference in good spirits you probably gave good feedback about it; if it ended with a dull speaker and a missed train your feedback may well be negative.

Whether we are involved or simply observers, we see things differently as a result of mood, expectation, distractions. If you're delivering a one-hour talk it will always feel longer and duller to you than for those listening, simply because you know the script. If someone tells you a movie is great, you're more likely to watch it appreciatively. If you're introduced to someone you've been warned is boring, you will probably be bored.

If everyone seems things slightly differently, imagine what our brain does with past events. Think about a sales presentation, for example. When you review your performance on the way home you're not assessing 100% of what happened, but selected moments. You're seeing the event through your eyes, not the eyes of your audience. Your perceptions are coloured by your feelings at the beginning and the end of the event, and by the closing remarks uttered as you were being ushered out of the room. How objectively are you summarizing a situation when you say 'that was a disaster'?

Reframing is about breaking out of habitual ways of thinking, putting aside assumptions and seeing new and old events from a very different perspective.

## TELL SOMEONE THE CLEAN FACTS

Next time you attend an event which relies on performance and interpersonal skills, e.g. a job interview or a business presentation, reframe the event rather than just doing a quick mental review on the way home. Most of the time we give ourselves a crude scoring somewhere between good, OK, and terrible. If it went well, how do you know, and how can you do even better next time by building on your strengths? If you feel it didn't go well, how do you know that's true, and which parts of your performance can you improve?

Tell someone what happened, not how you feel about it. As far as possible repeat the words you used and the order you did things. Talk about the questions you received and what, exactly, you said in reply. Talk about the reactions you actually heard, not those you sensed. Describe the event as if you had been an observer. You still won't present a totally objective picture, but by focusing on the facts you'll take a great deal of emotional colour out of your memory and you will learn more.

When you have described each stage of the event, ask for questions from your supporter, focusing again on what actually happened. Only when you have done this in detail should you allow yourself to talk about how you feel – you'll find in fact that this matters less now as you can really focus on doing things differently in the future.

## RETHINK THE WORD 'MISTAKE'

As the experiences of South Africa and Northern Ireland arguably teach us, societies move on best from conflict not just through peacekeeping but through honest reconciliation. In short, we stop killing each other when we start to accept that other people see the world differently, when we make an active choice to put the past behind us, and when we allow mistakes to become past events rather than current obsessions.

Cutting yourself some slack is about personal peace-making; accepting yourself, forgiving yourself. We have to make mistakes because human beings learn best (sometimes) from painful experiment; you learn to run elegantly by falling on your face in the most comical way imaginable.

Accept that your mistakes, even the ones that make you cringe, are an important part of who you are. Strength comes naturally to some, to others it's built from layers of vulnerability, one experience layered over another. That is one very important kind of resilience, a kind of body armour built from experience, whether good, bad, or indifferent. As the old saying goes, what doesn't kill you makes you stronger.

## STAND IN SOMEONE ELSE'S SHOES FOR A WHILE

Improving your resilience in a work context is often about anticipating conflict, and it's more predictable than we like to admit. Think about difficult conversations not just in terms of what will be said, but also how it will be said. How will the person on the receiving end feel afterwards?

Some highly effective managers spend a lot of time thinking about how colleagues will hear what they plan to say (see Chapter 24). They ask themselves and others about the likely reaction, and the likely outcome. You may have colleagues around you who like to drop bombshells into a conversation and then express complete (and often unconvincing) surprise when colleagues become upset.

Anticipating how others will react requires emotional intelligence and a good people 'radar'. If your experience firmly indicates that you don't do this well, borrow someone else's. Find someone who's really good with people and say 'if I say this to Bill, how do you think he will respond?'.

Walking in others' shoes isn't just about difficult messages. Anything high profile you do at work shapes the way others see you, and if you're going to stay ahead of the curve you need to check in regularly on the way you are seen by others. A mentor will help (see Chapter 38), but an important resilience strategy is to check out now and again how others perceive you. Don't overdo this, but take key opportunities two or three times a year to find out how colleagues see your contribution.

### Putting it all together

The word 'reframing' might remind us of the visual arts. Every painting and photograph has a frame, even if this is just the edge of the paper. The frame's position is no accident; where the image begins and ends is an important artistic decision. The image-maker has decided what to include and what to leave out, and that's a statement. Framing is always about selecting.

Some of these frames are shaped by habit alone: photographs, PowerPoint slides, and pieces of office paper come in defined proportions, known as aspect ratios. For example, we are used to seeing pictures which fit the 3:2 aspect ratio of 35 mm film, or the 4:3 ratio of many computer monitors. We frame things by habit more often than by choice or design.

Similarly, we look at experience through 'frames': we shape our memories so they make sense. We remember incidents that fit our picture of ourselves, and forget those that don't. We frame perception through our expectation of how things will be in the future. On the other hand, entirely new data can shake us up. When new perceptions break through strongly enough to challenge preconceptions, we are surprised. Just think of those times someone sent you on a training course that you thought would be dull and it turned out to be inspirational.

Reframing isn't about seeing the past through rose-tinted glasses, or sweeping errors under the carpet. It's about stepping back to discover if there is another way of seeing things.

# 6 Get out of victim mode

**GG** *'Self-pity is easily the most destructive of the non-pharmaceutical narcotics; it is addictive, gives momentary pleasure and separates the victim from reality.'* John Gardner

**GG** *'Take your life in your own hands, and what happens? A terrible thing: no one to blame.'* Erica Jong

**GG** *'Wise people learn not to dread but actually to welcome problems because it is in this whole process of meeting and solving problems that life has its meaning.'* M. Scott Peck

**GG** *'Action springs not from thought, but from a readiness for responsibility.'* Dietrich Bonhoeffer

**GG** *'Respect only has meaning as respect for those with whom I do not agree.'* Karen Armstrong

Whether you feel in charge of life or feel that life is in charge of you (see Chapter 13 on locus of control), the interesting thing is that you'll find it easy to turn up evidence which can confirm either belief system. In the words of resilience expert Al Siebert: 'both sets of beliefs are self-validating and self-fulfilling. People who believe that their fate is under the control of outside forces act in ways that confirm their beliefs. People who know they can do things to make life batter act in ways that confirm their beliefs' (*The Resiliency Advantage,* Berrett-Koehler, 2005).

Situations create victims for external or internal reasons, or a mixture of both. If someone decides to persecute or bully you,

29

that makes you – objectively – a victim in the sense of being on the receiving end of certain behaviours. However you can put yourself in the position of victim for a range of reasons. Some people feel marginalized by technological change, for example, or because they didn't go to university. Others may feel victimized by one business decision.

We choose to become, and remain, victims. Those who do so often have a fatalistic view of life. Every solution is met with a barrage of 'yes, but …' answers. A long queue of people have tried to help without success. Such individuals often fail to commit to goals which will assist their well-being, and sometimes engineer new situations which reinforce their sense of failure.

Self-appointed victims sometimes go out of their way to perpetuate negative working environments. Unconsciously they seem to do things which irritate and by doing so attract bad behaviour in others. Then, sadly, they sometimes inflict the same pain on others. They feel trapped and powerless, and yet – paradoxically – expend a huge amount of creative energy. Such self-defeating behaviours are paradoxically imaginative: a huge amount of creativity is needed in order to maintain victim mode.

Don't act out life as if it's a soap opera script. Watch out for impulses and, worse still, actions which begin with *poor me*.

## STOP LOOKING FOR VILLAINS AND WHITE KNIGHTS

In the late 1960s psychiatrist Stephen Karpman created a triangular model to describe human interaction. He based it on narrative structures in traditional fairy tales:

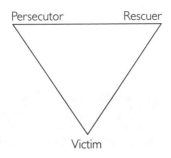

Persecutor          Rescuer

Victim

The model draws on age-old themes of hero, villain and someone vulnerable in distress. Here the roles of Persecutor, Rescuer and Victim are given capital letters to show that they are roles we adopt rather than real-life contexts. The model provides insights into the way people see themselves and others in situations involving tension or conflict. People see themselves as victim in a situation because they feel they have no control. If they have no control, logically they seek an external source for their distress – a persecutor. This may be real, imagined, or a mixture of both. So if you've just been turned down for a promotion on the grounds that your skills are not up to date, you may decide to blame your line manager or training team.

Finding a persecutor in this model is often less about spotting someone who is actively plotting your downfall, but finding someone to blame. The unhappy victim then seeks a rescuer, but will often in fact not respond to positive interventions or advice. Alternatively, you may see yourself in rescuer mode, taking on responsibility when someone should be doing something for themselves. Rescuers often have mixed motives.

The Karpman triangle shows how we create complex everyday fantasies to avoid moving towards an internal locus of control. When things have gone wrong for you, how often have you placed responsibility for the situation – and responsibility for solving it – in the hands of others?

## DON'T CHOOSE VICTIM MODE

Being the victim in a situation is strangely comforting. You allow yourself to feel sad, dejected, beaten up. You privately enjoy your little revenge fantasies. You find yourself eating comfort food. You take things out on your work colleagues or family – why shouldn't they experience some of the stuff dished out to you?

Breaking out of victim mode can provoke something which feels like bereavement, because you're putting this childlike state aside, and no one likes saying goodbye to childhood.

Start to redirect all the creative, spiteful, twisted energy you put into being a victim into just being a fairly ordinary person dealing with ordinary situations. Playing the victim card all the time is often about saying 'look at me', and always about watching for further slights, knock-backs and evil scheming.

To stop being a victim, start by being very clear about the one person who's responsible for the way you feel: you. This is of course uncomfortable, and it's tempting to start blaming yourself for not taking responsibility. Breaking out of old thinking is about finding equilibrium rather than blame, looking at the things you have some control over and ignoring the rest (see Chapter 14).

Don't try to do things alone – see below.

## IMPORT SOME OBJECTIVITY

Resist the temptation to turn life into fairy tales (or old-school Westerns with white and black hats to differentiate good from bad). This often starts by you deciding not to blame anyone, including yourself.

It's a tough call to look at any situation objectively when you're involved in it, so find someone who isn't. Find someone who is calm, not likely to jump to conclusions, and not in any way involved in the problem or any outcomes. When you sit down with your trusted colleague, you both need to commit to three things:

1. No blame. You may decide later where cause and responsibility lie, but at the outset you'll both resist the temptation to allocate fault.
2. Look at feelings first, getting them aired and out of the way, agreeing that neither of you will draw conclusions from them.
3. You will then look at the facts, describing the situation in calm language that a fair and reasonable outside observer would use.

All this moves towards 'clean' language (see Chapter 5) which is less cluttered with emotional content, helps to clarify the real facts, and starts to look at what has gone on as something which can be managed if you choose to try out new approaches and behaviours.

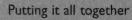

## Putting it all together

Acknowledging how often you are trapped by victim mode is a major step towards sustained resilience. It teaches you to look at past events not in terms of persecution and defeat, but as learning opportunities allowing you to build your own resources. Recognizing your need for a Rescuer also provides insights into your self-efficacy (see Chapter 11).

Stepping away from victim mode means that you can start to examine your hurt feelings rather than being driven by them. Now you will also look at facts and contexts. You start to see how other people think and what may have motivated their actions. You will probably discover that they weren't out to get you; and if they really are, that's also good to know as well.

If you spend hours each week focused on the victim hand you've been dealt, it's time you played those cards out and started a new game. Look hard at how you frame experience in terms of overriding narratives ('why does this always happen to me?') and where you place others in your story ('why does my boss always ignore my suggestions?').

Attend to facts, not to the way you have shaped them to fit your prejudices. Stop expecting rescuers to arrive over the horizon on white chargers. If you need to change the way you do things, start that change.

Try asking questions that begin with the positive assumption that things are already pretty good. Perhaps the first should be 'why am I so lucky?'

# 7 Learn from past bounce-backs

> 'The only real mistake is the one from which we learn nothing.'
> Henry Ford

> 'Turn your wounds into wisdom.' Oprah Winfrey

> 'The past is never where you think you left it.' Katherine Anne Porter

> 'Life is very interesting. In the end, some of your greatest pains become your greatest strengths.' Drew Barrymore

> 'As long as the world is turning and spinning, we're gonna be dizzy and we're gonna make mistakes.' Mel Brooks

San Diego psychologist Mark Katz runs the 'Resilience Through The Life Span' project. Like others he wonders why some people not only survive childhood adversity but go on to thrive in later life. However he also wonders why some troubled people who have suffered life adjustment problems for years reach a sudden breakthrough later in life and achieve a complete turnaround. Katz suggests that such experience is about feeling mastery over circumstances and ourselves. Katz's mantra, often quoted in child psychology, is 'there is never anything wrong with us that something right with us can't fix'.

Turning point experiences of this kind vary enormously. For some it's a reading a book or hearing a motivational speaker. Others include strong relationships, new learning opportunities, or having a mentor or coach. Experience provides all kinds of learning, particularly when we reframe things (see Chapter 5). This learning can sometimes be a slow burn where things are processed gradually. Occasionally we have sudden moments of insight where our past makes sense. This can be provoked by crisis. When everything is going well we generally repeat safe behaviours and don't need to learn much, but when things go wrong we can gain new insights.

When individuals present to coaches in a state of helplessness they have often closed a heavy bulkhead door on their own past. Straightforward questions such as 'where have you dealt with a dilemma like this before?' and 'what strategies have you used to overcome this problem in the past?' can unlock evidence of past resourcefulness.

One effect of anxiety and stress is to force a particular view of past, present and future. Your caught-in-the-headlights brain sees no immediate choices, anticipates a future which involves only loss or pain, and has no use for your past (except perhaps to run a narrative that says 'you've always been rubbish at this').

The past is rich territory. You probably have dealt with something similar in the past, even if it was just the same emotional state. Activating your memory can provide firm evidence of that fact that you've been resilient before, and can be again.

## TACKLE EXTERNAL CONSTRAINTS CREATIVELY

If you're feeling boxed in, look at those external factors which constrain you. These could be location (you need to limit your commute or need to live in a particular location), time (you need flexible working), financial commitments, absolute barriers in your work environment (e.g. software platforms or market regulations) or other issues such as access to information (e.g. you can't access old contact lists used in a previous role).

These are external constraints in the sense that they exist independently of you, no matter how you feel about them. Even if such constraints are highly restrictive, at least you know the rules of the game. Your response to them can of course vary enormously, from a fatalistic 'I'm hemmed in' to a flexible-minded 'how do I make this work?'.

Let's say, for example, that you are blocked in promotion terms and not earning enough, and your external network is not strong enough to help you find a role elsewhere. A passive approach would be to keep your head down, an active one would be to work creatively at expanding your role while building up your external network by information gathering or sharing.

Knowing what external constraints you face now, ask yourself where you have overcome them in the past (see below).

## BE HONEST ABOUT INTERNAL CONSTRAINTS

Internal constraints are more about you than the environment. So although you're talking about market forces (e.g. 'employers don't like generalists' or 'I'm held back by my lack of a degree') the real constraining factor may be your assumptions.

Internal constraints are largely about confidence and the need to maintain a smaller, safer picture of yourself than you need to project. So accepting the self-defining statement 'I'm not a people person' is a way of avoiding the risk of developing some modest people skills and trying them out. Internal constraints are more powerful than external ones because they act as blinkers; you prevent yourself from seeing options and solutions, and make yourself unable even to begin problem solving. It's as if you constantly check potential actions against a badly-drawn uncomplimentary portrait painted by someone who dislikes you intensely.

## REDISCOVER PAST STRENGTHS

See constraints as nothing new, whether they are external or internal. Look at how you got over, under or past them on earlier occasions. For example, if your path is blocked because you lack a particular qualification or training experience, look at times in your past when you talked yourself into a role by emphasizing your skills and experience rather than your academic achievement.

You can learn even more from past recoveries, whether from disaster or disappointment. The main reason for doing so is to challenge any feelings you have of powerlessness. Remembering that you have been this way before gives you access to tried and tested solutions.

The advantage of reviewing things in hindsight is that you look back through the lens of known outcomes. You process the story not from the position of feeling beaten up and without choices as you feel now, but knowing how it ended. Even if the conclusion wasn't entirely positive, the significant facts are that you got through it, and you are better equipped now to deal with the problem than you were then. Don't let panic convince you that you're facing completely unknown challenges.

Spend more than a moment reviewing how you overcame problems which seriously unbalanced your confidence. Look at what you did, step by step. If you recovered your gravitas, sense of humour, or gained a valuable sense of perspective, how did you do it? Look back on the personal resources you drew out in those moments, and how you sustained courage and determination under fire (or at least hung on in there).

Now, thinking about the same past experiences, dig deep in memory to identify the moment when the wind changed, the moment when you rediscovered the path and found confidence. What was the turning point? If it was a conversation with someone supportive, recreate that environment. If it was simply about taking some time out to gather facts and do some thinking, repeat that strategy.

### Putting it all together

Habits form easily, and one of the most uninspiring is making each day predictably free of risk and mistakes. As Chapter 2 shows, mistakes allow you to fail forwards. You also learn from more dramatic forms of recovery – not just from mistakes, but from confidence-denting setbacks. You can rediscover resilience in your present by learning from times you demonstrated or acquired it in your past.

Start by looking objectively at the problems you face today, putting clear blue water between external constraints that are largely things you have to live with, and internal constraints which are the shackles you put in place to limit your own performance.

Look more closely at problems that seem overwhelming and leave you feeling powerless. How much of your dilemma is a persistent belief that you're facing something you've never experienced before? This is unlikely to be true. With a bit of lateral thinking you can start to remember times when you summoned inner resources to dig yourself out of a hole, and you can do it again.

Look hard, therefore, at the things that prevent you from moving forward. How many of them are genuinely external constraints – and how much of the time are you getting in the way of yourself? How many barriers are of your own making?

When it comes to rediscovering even the smallest shreds of resilience, your past is a great teacher. Thinking about past events and turning points enables you to remember not just that you succeeded in the past but how you did it.

# 8 Blame yourself only when you can learn something

66 'A mistake is not something to be determined after the fact, but in the light of the information until that point.'
Nassim Nicholas Taleb

66 'Don't look where you fell, look where you slipped.'
African proverb

66 'Who can really say how decisions are made, how emotions change, how ideas arise? We talk about inspiration; about a bolt of lightning from a clear sky, but perhaps everything is just as simple and just as infinitely complex as the processes that make a particular leaf fall at a particular moment. That point has been reached, that's all. It has to happen, and it does happen.'
John Ajvide Lindqvist

66 'It is only through labour and painful effort, by grim energy and resolute courage, that we move on to better things.'
Theodore Roosevelt

66 'Accepting trial and error means accepting error. It means taking problems in our stride when a decision doesn't work out, whether through luck or misjudgement. And that is not something human brains seem to be able to do without a struggle.' Tim Harford

When people don't acknowledge their mistakes, that may signal arrogance, but more frequently it means they are blind to them and will keep on making them. When they do accept that their behaviours have caused problems, blame usually kicks in. Sometimes this is essentially about subtly shifting the blame ('I would have got it right if ...'), and at other times they simply beat themselves up.

A phrase that has emerged in business life in recent years is the expression 'put your hands up for', to indicate 'owning up to'. It is usually swiftly followed by the word 'but' offering some form of justification. It reflects insecurity, and perhaps a little caution; people are dismissed for all kinds of reasons, so taking absolute blame for anything is potentially dangerous.

Blame and shame are strongly linked. Blame is the public face, shame the private one. However, both are guilt-inducing triggers that can distract you from the real value of mistakes: what you learn from them. The fact that someone or something has been blamed is usually very little to do with facts, and much more in the realm of wild hunches or finger-pointing. When the teacher questions you in the playground you instinctively want to point to someone else, but on the way home you blame yourself both for the action you failed to admit and for betraying a classmate.

Blame is a hungry beast; it requires feeding. When you blame yourself for something that's not a momentary thought, but a minor obsession likely to last hours, if not days. Blame requires you to re-run events in your head, to keep asking yourself why you didn't say or do something different.

One aspect of blame we find difficult to acknowledge is that it is peculiarly addictive. It may not be enjoyable, but it is a place in your mind and memory where you may choose to dwell, rather like running your finger over a cut or bruise, wincing at the memory of the original injury.

## ACCEPT RESPONSIBILITY, PUT BLAME ASIDE

There is an important difference between blaming yourself and taking responsibility. Blame is a childlike response about channelling contempt or ridicule; taking responsibility is an adult response framed around a shared understanding that things go wrong for a wide variety of factors. Blame points at one person, responsibility points at contexts.

When you accept responsibility, you are giving objective feedback that you were part of a context. It doesn't mean that you are the sole cause of a problem. If you made an arithmetical error when you were tired, for example, it could be because your workload has been pushed beyond reasonable limits, or because the system didn't provide checks and balances to allow for predictable mistakes.

Blame is often disconnected from facts (see Chapter 4). Be clear about what has happened and what the impact was before playing the blame game. You may learn a lot from a mistake that has only light consequences (it's called a near miss).

Blame can be about asking the unanswerable questions we ask our children: 'why did you do that? What were you thinking of?' Accepting responsibility is about looking to the future and deciding what can be fixed now and improved later, and so is about asking 'what were the early warning signs here that this wasn't a good decision?' and 'how can we avoid this next time?'

Responsibility is about accepting a duty of care and a duty of self-examination. It is about honestly accepting the fact of the error. This is important: if you have glossed over your mistake, diminished its impact, partially blamed others, you are still trying to hide the reality from yourself. A resilient response to mistakes is about full acceptance, learning, and moving on.

## LOOK BACK IN FORGIVENESS

It's entertaining to attribute fault. It makes life more like soap opera to find the villain in every situation, but as the expression goes, s**t happens. Each journey has its uphill sections.

Try letting things go. Only worry about the big issues, the things that really matter. You may discover that most things don't really matter all that much. You can prove this to yourself by reviewing past blame crises: times at least a year ago when you lost sleep and huge amounts of self-confidence by blaming yourself for mistakes. Think about the events and issues concerned. How much do these things matter now? How quickly were they forgotten or swept aside by other events?

Fear and panic come from somewhere in your primeval brain which is capable of paralysing your whole body. All kinds of physical responses are triggered including increased pulse, breathing, digestive disorders and blushing; in extreme situations these can easily prevent people speaking and thinking. Your primitive brain is looking for a 'fight or flight' moment, and this heightened response puts your entire focus on here and now. It's hard to think ahead to consequences, which is why we make even more mistakes if we give in to instinctive responses under stress (see Chapter 37).

However, looking back at these events enables you to see them as part of a bigger picture, and you will generally see that what seemed like a life-and-death matter at the time will be revealed as what a colleague of mine described as 'normal small business stuff'.

## EASE UP

Blaming yourself for nearly everything that comes along means that you have unconsciously adopted a posture you intend to repeat: one of weakness and humility. You have trained yourself to deflect the risk of criticism by inflicting it on yourself. Your first reaction is cowed, like a dog faced down by a larger beast.

Resilient behaviour is about preparing yourself for tough situations; blaming yourself all the time easily shifts you into victim mode (see Chapter 6), expecting life to give you a hard time and then licking your wounds in a 'told you so' state of mind.

If you are blaming yourself for most things that go wrong, this might also be a form of self-indulgence. It's certainly lazy thinking, avoiding real investigation into how things happen and what could be done to change things. It's a great way of denying your potential or closing the doors to possible learning.

### Putting it all together

Blame is the easiest tool to reach in a crisis. It's right there under the lid of the toolkit, with a bright luminous handle. Yes, it's the fire axe, the large and dangerous red object you start swinging when the house is burning. Some people sink the axe into the woodwork just when they smell smoke.

Blame is a deep-down, primary response that's about finding a place of safety out of the gaze of the predator. *Don't look at me – look over there. Eat him first – he's slower and fatter.* We are tremendously creative when it comes to avoiding being prey. *I wasn't there, you say. It can't have been me.*

However your next instinct might be to say *It's all my fault. Don't punish me.* Denial and self-deprecation are closely linked. Sometimes you accept blame tentatively in the hope that others will tell you it's not your fault, but this can easily misfire. Another variation is that you own up in a way that passes the buck: *I hadn't been trained properly. You didn't give me the resources. You drove me to it.* This blame transference reveals a very passive approach close to victim status.

If you're being too hard on yourself, it's likely that you are also too critical of others around you, seeing threats rather than collaboration, rivals rather than colleagues.

Blame is a weapon, especially if you turn it on yourself. It can damage reputations, fracture relationships. Use sparingly, and with caution.

## 9 Don't listen to 2 a.m. voices

> 'Never be bullied into silence. Never allow yourself to be made a victim. Accept no one's definition of your life; define yourself.'
> Harvey Fierstein

> 'Every thought is a seed. If you plant crab apples, don't count on harvesting Golden Delicious.' Bill Meyer

> 'Defeat is not bitter unless you swallow it.' Joe Clark

> 'Success is not final, failure is not fatal: it is the courage to continue that counts.' Winston Churchill

> 'The reason why worry kills more people than work is that more people worry than work.' Robert Frost

Even if you're not an insomniac, there will be times when you find yourself awake in the middle of the night, with things on your mind. Have you noticed how small issues become big concerns at two or three o'clock in the morning (or whatever hour of darkness you find yourself awake and worrying)? You might find yourself worrying about things that are coming up the next day, such as a difficult meeting or presentation. You might be reviewing the day that has just gone, regretting things that happened. Before long your mind drifts into bigger concerns: everything that isn't working out for you.

Soon you're hearing self-talk; those voices in your head describing you in ways you don't want to hear. You know these middle-of-the-night voices. The ones that tell you that you're too old, not smart enough, too dull, too unattractive. Sometimes you hear real words, at other times it's more like seeing yourself in a mirror.

The more these voices echo round your head, the more seriously you take them. After all, there's nothing else to hear or think about. They can easily fill your head so you can't think anything else.

Be careful what you listen to. This self-talk may sometimes be regretful – what you should have said and done – but often it's just negative statements about yourself, taking one event and using it as an excuse to label yourself for ever. Listen carefully to the words that come up in that self-talk; what you allow your brain to say about you, and how you listen to it.

You might get up and write things down. More worrying still, you might *do* something, translating feelings into decisions and actions. Most decisions made at this time of night say 'no' rather than 'yes'. They are about escape or avoidance: decisions to give up, get out, run away. It's no surprise – the lonely human in the depths of the night is drawing on ancient instincts focused on safety and risk avoidance. The cornered animal wants either to find a quick exit, or to surrender.

## DON'T GIVE THE MIDNIGHT VOICES AN OPEN MICROPHONE

One characteristic of repeated, troubling thoughts is that they love taking you round in circles. You try to bend them into straight lines leading to solutions, but by nature they want to spin round, repeating themselves in endless thought loops.

As the questions and 'what ifs' go round, you may start to voice answers, but be careful of the temptation to voice things to others. Some of the most damaging voicemails are recorded at the wrong end of the day.

Writing things down can help you see some light. Many people find it therapeutic to write 'to-do' lists or to set out pros and cons. If that works for you and makes it easier for you to get back to sleep, go for it (see also Chapter 10 on using this as a technique to postpone worrying). It's best to write things down in a notebook beside your bed rather than booting up your computer or iPad; once you do that you can easily switch into action mode when you start sending out emails (you'll also stay awake: screen light discourages sleep).

Writing things down is often a good way of clearing the brain out. If you do need a keyboard (perhaps because fine-tuning the language in a document will help you think straight), then power up your computer (just don't do anything with the text you produce – the most career-damaging emails are the sent at 2 a.m.).

Even if you think you're producing reasonable text and not an angry rant while the world dozes, approach the task with supreme care. For example, don't compose an email using your normal software. Write it out separately, for example in a Word document, not in an email message; it's all too easy in a sleep-deprived state to press 'send' accidentally and to broadcast a message that you know will sound like a fit of pique or crazed nonsense when you read it at breakfast time.

## CHECK OUT THE CARTOON

You don't just listen to words in the middle of the night, you paint a new self-portrait. It's not a pretty sight. Look carefully and critically at that picture. It will almost certainly be a cartoon version of you. It's you, but with all your strengths diminished, and your flaws exaggerated. The cracks in your façade look like chasms.

Step back and look at this negative picture of yourself. See how comical it is. Look at it closely and you will have to admit that it is no more real than any caricature. The best way of not taking this cartoon picture of you seriously is to exaggerate it further. If your picture shows you being unprepared for a critical meeting, imagine not turning up at all and going to the beach instead. Try making the picture look even worse and you will see that your 2 a.m. mind sees only lurid cartoons, not reality.

# STEP BACK A LITTLE

The best antidote to 2 a.m. voices, apart from sleep, is a bit of objectivity.

Time provides a good sense of perspective. Most problems evaporate, or at least become manageable, within 48 hours. If you're worried in the wee small hours of Thursday, imagine how you will feel on Saturday afternoon. Imagine all the other trivial things that will come along and force this issue off your agenda. Remember that the vast majority of things we lie awake and worry about go away on their own, or seem insignificant or irrelevant as other things happen (see Chapter 10 on worry).

It may also help to imagine the problem as much bigger than it is. If you've bounced a cheque, for example, imagine how you would feel if you were bankrupt. If you've offended someone, imagine how you'd feel if you had done so in public. If you sent an email you regret, think about how you'd feel if you had commissioned posters with the same message. Build it up and then see that the problem you really have to deal with is smaller, and much more manageable.

## Putting it all together

Psychologists tell us that the voice speaking to us in the middle of the night is the voice of a child. This idea contains an important truth. You believe you are listening to an adult brain processing events, choices, dilemmas, but the noises you are hearing are more about distress and anxiety than they are about real issues. You may think you are weighing up choices, but your mind has been temporarily hijacked by a tired, hurt child.

No matter how grown-up you think you feel during the day, the anxious voice you hear is the voice of a frightened child speaking to itself in the darkness, when every problem looks bigger than it is, and the morning seems a long way off.

If you accept that 2 a.m. words are spoken by a child, then do what you would do if a child was worried at that hour of the morning: listen, and be a voice of comfort, but don't act upon what you hear. Observe how you feel (write down your reflections and feelings if that helps, trying to describe them accurately as if you were observing someone else).

Whatever your 2 a.m. voices say to you, don't act on impulse, don't fire off an email or leave a phone message, and above all else don't make a decision, because you're in entirely the wrong place to do any of those things. It will be a vulnerable and frightened child doing the deciding.

# 10 Stop worrying

**"** *'Stop worrying… nobody gets out of this world alive.'* Clive James

**"** *'Worry does not empty tomorrow of its sorrow, it empties today of its strength.'* Corrie ten Boom

**"** *'Do not anticipate trouble, or worry about what may never happen. Keep in the sunlight.'* Benjamin Franklin

**"** *'The most important thing is not to think very much about oneself. To investigate candidly the charge; but not fussily, not very anxiously. On no account to retaliate by going to the other extreme – thinking too much.'* Virginia Woolf

**"** *'I am an old man and have known a great many troubles, but most of them have never happened.'* Mark Twain

Although some children worry, it's something we get to be *really* good at later in life. We are largely trained to worry – it's rarely a natural trait. As we approach adulthood we are taught that we should be worrying about examination results, earning a living, looking good, having an appropriate social media profile. We are conditioned that worry is a grown-up activity, and that it is purposeful and constructive.

Worry is overrated. We associate it with real fear, such as our 'fight or flight' mechanism. This is about real danger, not worrying what people at the office are saying about you. The problem is that these thought mechanisms seem to overlap. When people experience highly traumatic events the details of the time, place, even the weather conditions at the time, stay with them. Our brains associate danger with the threat of predators, so it's a useful survival mechanism to remember details for a long time. However this also seems to result in an ability to worry about imagined dangers with similar intensity, and worry is far less useful than danger-mapping.

Worrying about a problem and thinking that problem through are very different processes. Worry is driven by fear, nightmare scenarios, and a cartoon picture of your worst self in operation (see Chapter 9). Problem-solving is about acknowledging emotional responses and putting them aside so you can look at solid facts. Getting even one part of the problem sorted is often a good way forward, simply because you're switching modes.

Since we have conditioned ourselves that worrying is akin to being responsible, we start to believe that the things we worry about are the most important matters. That's why you leave your wallet at home on a day when you're thinking about a difficult meeting, and why it's easier to lose your way in a presentation if you've just read an unrelated but troubling email five minutes before you start. Learn to recognize your triggers and blind spots.

Since worry is so thoroughly conditioned, the solution cannot be about being obsessive or worrying about how much worrying we do.

Watch out also for actions driven by restlessness, or fear of missing out (FOMO in Twitter-speak). This isn't just anxiety about not having the latest gadget, but a state where you find it hard to enjoy what you're doing because you're anxious that something more exciting is happening elsewhere.

## POSTPONE WORRYING

One school of therapy suggests that you postpone worry until a time when you can deal with it better. It's easier to postpone worry than to exclude it from your mind.

Recognize early signs of worry, the things that might trigger this for you (for example if your bank balance hits rock bottom, or when you spend too much time on your own, or at certain times of day or night).

Make a diary note to worry at a time of day when you know you are more positive. Just write down one phrase such as 'bank loan' or 'assignment'. You're making a deal with yourself to come back and think about the subject when you are in a better state of mind. When the time comes, do the worrying. Sometimes it helps to have a set time and place where you will do this. Worrying when you're calmer will often mean that problems seem much smaller and solutions more obvious.

Some therapists suggest that you can even keep postponing these worry sessions indefinitely. This allows you repeated opportunities to build in a delay between impulse and action. Others suggest that you get to grips with what's worrying you and let it play out – see below.

## PUSH THE WORST-CASE SCENARIO

In your worry time (see above) focus on one issue only. Since you have found a time when you are likely to think about the topic more optimistically, you might be tempted to jump straight to solutions. However, try over-examining the dark side first.

Ask yourself 'what's the worst that could happen?'. Push that question to irrational limits: write down your worst fear and the worst possible outcome, no matter how unrealistic. Visualize this worst-case scenario in detail. Don't try to push aside any feelings of anxiety, but dwell in them for a while.

Psychologists tell us that 'worry expression', allowing your anxieties your full attention for about 25–30 minutes, naturally causes them to weaken, through a process described as *habituation*. In other words, your brain becomes bored with them, which has long-term benefits (while 'worry suppression', pushing feelings down or trying to distracting yourself, works only in the short term). Allowing yourself to experience anxious thoughts fully, repeatedly and at length, surprisingly robs them of their power.

# STOP WORRYING ABOUT WORRYING

Most people worry, and most worry is irrational, as this chapter reveals. The problem comes when we upgrade these passing fears into important obsessions. A moment of self-doubt is just a moment. When we build it into a system it becomes the centre point of attention and energy.

Start to think about moments of anxiety and even fear of small glitches. Don't analyse, because this supports your obsessions. The problem here isn't about content, but about how you are reacting. We pretend that analysing helps us to get to the root cause or find solutions, but in reality we start to think in circles. Soon you are worrying about worry itself. Equally, don't try to work out what these responses 'mean', and don't worry about whether they will go away.

Since the aim is to achieve a state of equilibrium, be honest about the fact that a passing thought has become a worry, and worrying is becoming obsessive. Remind yourself that momentary obsessions are normal, but the obsession part of it is the least important aspect. Don't start analysing or over-processing, and watch out if you begin linking this worry to all the other worries you have; this is a great way of seeing negative patterns that don't really exist.

Do something that helps you change your emotional response. Write down any images or impulses that come to mind. Writing them down reveals that they are irrational statements of fear. You start to recognize how repetitive and senseless these reactions are. Through repetition these ideas start to lose their power. Use the worst-case scenario technique described above.

Finally, modify the picture. If your worry is seeing yourself in a state of ill health, or unemployment, play a different movie: you as a fighting fit and fully employed individual. Force a shift from negative to positive feelings.

## Putting it all together

We all worry, in large or small doses. Worrying, and how we deal with it, is closely related to resilience. Worry has a function but needs keeping it in its place.

Worry unbalances and destabilizes by painting negative pictures as if they are reality. Actions driven by worry are often just a cry for help; real prioritizing and planning is about seeing the difference between what you feel and what can be done. The best strategies to counteract worry are often ways of tricking your mind to let go, postpone, or sideline worry.

Think about the tremendous amounts of psychological energy that go into worry and anxiety. What would it be like for you if that energy went into other kinds of expression? What would you working week be like, for example, if you spent as much time imagining and planning optimistically?

Psychologists remind us that worry has the perverse effect of drawing us towards the thing we want to avoid. If you're climbing a ladder and worry obsessively about falling off, it becomes more likely that you do so. If you're worried about singing out of tune, worry constrains your voice. If you worry hard enough about missing a penalty kick, you'll probably miss it.

Don't confuse worry or anxiety with planning. Worrying about an interview, for example, is not the same as preparing for one. Ironically, worry prevents good preparation; because you don't want to visualize a future event, you fail to imagine what you should do and say when it comes along.

# Rethink the way you set goals

> ❝ *'I can't fix the world. If you want to make a difference in life, you have to direct your energies in a focused way.'* Bill Bryson

> ❝ *'We aim above the mark to hit the mark.'* Ralph Waldo Emerson

> ❝ *'Our plans miscarry because they have no aim. When a man does not know what harbour he is making for, no wind is the right wind.'* Seneca

> ❝ *'Only those who will risk going too far can possibly find out how far one can go.'* T. S. Eliot

> ❝ *'A goal properly set is halfway reached.'* Abraham Lincoln

At one time we believed that low self-esteem in children caused mental health problems. Now we see self-esteem as an evident spin-off of resilience. Feeling that we are competent and capable of making a contribution naturally helps us see ourselves as having value. Child psychologists often now focus less on generalized encouragement ('believe in yourself - you can do anything'), and more on helping young people gain a realistic sense of their own abilities and then reinforcing experiences of achievement ('persist and you will achieve something worthwhile').

Much of this is linked to the theory of self-efficacy, characterized by Professor Albert Bandura as 'the belief in one's capabilities to organize and execute the courses of action required to manage prospective situations'. Self-efficacy therefore describes your belief in your ability to succeed in a particular situation. In

2004 Bandura showed how self-efficacy based beliefs produced positive results in people who suffered from severe debilitating trauma such as natural disaster or wartime experience. Where subjects felt they had some control over their traumatic experience, veterans and hurricane survivors were able to overcome distress and move towards productive activity.

People with strong self-efficacy view challenges as problems to be solved or tasks to be completed, and so recover more quickly from setbacks and disappointments. People with a weak sense of self-efficacy tend to avoid challenging tasks, believing these are beyond their capabilities, and lose confidence in their competence.

A key stage in this process is believing that goals are worth setting and will have useful outcomes. We are all entertained by fantasy futures; we love to talk about dream scenarios such as winning the lottery or being able to retire early on a private income. These are fantasies, not goals, because they are essentially passive: you hope that something will come along to change your life. Goal setting is about adopting a very simple belief – the changes that will improve your life will happen because you engineer them in some way (see Chapter 13 on internal locus of control).

## FOLLOW ACTION PLANS, NOT MYTHS

There is a pervasive idea in circulation which says that if you write down a goal you measurably improve the chances that it will come true. For some it seems that if you put the wildest goal on paper and believe in it with sufficient fervour, that will make it happen.

Richard Wiseman, in his myth-busting *59 Seconds,* shows there is no evidence supporting this claim. Yet it is repeated widely on the internet and by motivational speakers, who sometimes suggest that academic research supports the concept (some cite studies conducted at Harvard in the 1950s, others research conducted at Yale in the 1970s. Neither institution has any record or knowledge of these programmes).

If you think about it, the idea is plain superstition, an ancient idea that mark-making will magically shape events. It is also distracting; writing the goal down becomes the answer, not taking action towards that goal. The myth encourages us to imagine goals which are so ambitious that we are relieved of any responsibility. For example, if your goal is to marry a millionaire, you can sit back and wait for fate to deliver.

Big goals need first steps. If your goal is to climb Mount Kilimanjaro, the most difficult step isn't the final one at the summit, but the first one you make tomorrow morning when you decide to talk to someone who has been there already.

## DO SWEAT THE SMALL STUFF

Richard Wiseman suggests that 88% of New Year's resolutions fail. It seems we are naturally attuned to over-promising and under-delivery when we set personal goals. However when we make goals small, specific and concrete, they are more demanding, because it becomes more obvious when we have done nothing about them. So *I must lose weight* simply induces a vague sense of guilt, but *I will stop eating desserts on weekdays* is focused and specific enough to help you form new habits.

Start by setting one step you can action immediately. Need to exercise? Set a first stage goal, e.g. deciding that whenever you park your car you will walk for at least 10 minutes before sitting. Break down large goals into small steps, mini-goals, and make those steps as simple to achieve as possible. Commit to them, recording progress methodically. Tell other people how you are doing: you receive support, help with setbacks, and you feel more accountable. If old habits kick in or things don't go to plan, see problems as temporary rather than an excuse to set your goals to one side.

B. J. Fogg of Stanford University's Persuasive Technology lab reveals (at www.tinyhabits.com) that there are only three ways you will make big changes. The first is that you have some kind of personal epiphany, which is fairly unlikely. The second is that you make changes to your environment, and the third is that you take small steps: tiny habits.

## GO BEYOND SMART

Countless business and self-help books will tell you to set goals that are SMART: usually expressed as specific, measurable, achievable, realistic, and time-bound. It's the bread and butter stuff of good planning. However it misses the human dimension. Why would you want to get out of your warm bed on a Monday morning to do something which was merely realistic or achievable (let alone measurable or time-bound, which sound really dull)? Find and set goals which are SMARTER: the E stands for Exciting, and the R sounds for rewarding.

If you can find something exciting in a plan, you're far more likely to follow it. Look at the difference, for example, between researching something 'just for work' and chasing information on a subject you are passionate about. Researching something which enlivens you means you're far more ready to accept setbacks and get past people who say 'no'.

'Rewarding' doesn't have to relate to money. Doing something rewarding means that there is an added tingle of motivation. You can make a mundane task more acceptable if you build in mini-rewards, like buying yourself a takeaway once you've done all the ironing or filled in your expenses.

### Putting it all together

Just as resilience is built by problem solving (see Chapter 13), it is strengthened by the ability to set goals and to work towards them. Goals are important because they are purposeful and help you anticipate setbacks.

Goal setting is about starting to take control of your circumstances and your environment. Accept one simple proposition about your life; most positive changes happen because you get involved. This might be because you make the change happen, or just that you see opportunities arrive. It may be that you make sure you don't get in the way when good things come along. The most important goal you can ever set is to take control of more of the things that shape your life so you rather than events write the script.

There is a huge amount of literature in the business world about how to set goals, but the most important step is the moment just after the goal is conceived. It is that moment when you decide to make things happen. Big goals are important because they push us beyond our comfort zones, but they are only useful to us if they offer an immediate, first step.

Don't set too many goals, because that will pretty much guarantee that none of them turn into reality. Rather than simply writing goals down, write down how you are going to move forward, step by step. Record your progress, and keep writing down descriptions of how life will be improved for you when your goal is achieved.

# 12 Get better at decision-making

**66** '*All our final decisions are made in a state of mind that is not going to last.*' Marcel Proust

**66** '*When it is not necessary to make a decision, it is necessary not to make a decision.*' Lucius Cary, Second Viscount Falkland

**66** '*Never cut a tree down in the wintertime. Never make a negative decision in the low time. Never make your most important decisions when you are in your worst moods. Wait. Be patient. The storm will pass. The spring will come.*' Robert H. Schuller

**66** '*It's the action, not the fruit of the action, that's important. You have to do the right thing. It may not be in your power, may not be in your time, that there will be any fruit. But that doesn't mean you stop doing the right thing. You may never know what results come from your action. But if you do nothing, there will be no result.*' Mahatma Gandhi

**66** '*On an important decision one rarely has 100% of the information needed for a good decision no matter how much one spends or how long one waits. And, if one waits too long, he has a different problem and has to start all over. This is the terrible dilemma of the hesitant decision-maker.*' Robert K. Greenleaf

The pace of life can be exhilarating, but it can also mean we miss the difference between critical and non-critical decisions. It's hardly ever productive to stress over small issues: your choice of take-away tonight probably won't matter much in the long run.

However, not finding the time to return a call from your former boss or failing to follow up on a great networking opportunity may be mistakes you can't undo.

Often people feel pressurized to make a decision before they are ready. You feel under pressure to make the right decision, but you don't really work in decision mode at all, just spin the issues around in your head. Eventually the pressure mounts so much that you simply make a decision just so the problem goes away. Often the worst decision is a simple 'yes': 'yes' to work overload, 'yes' to an underpaid project, 'yes' to volunteering just to please someone, 'yes' to accepting a poisoned chalice that everyone else has avoided.

Instincts are often helpful here, and the most important instinct is 'I'm not sure'. If something feels wrong, it probably won't work for you. Real wisdom however is to treat every important decision, attractive or unattractive, with the same caution. That doesn't mean that you have to sound cautious; you can buy time without making people feel you're suspicious or ungrateful.

Most decision-making is flawed, but that doesn't mean that we should avoid it. An important part of resilience is knowing when to make a decision on partial information. The American economists Baumol and Quandt coined the delightful phrase 'optimally imperfect decision' which looks at the marginal cost of gathering additional information or performing more refined calculations. Bookkeepers know this principle well: if your accounts are just a few pounds out of balance, it will cost you to less to simply write off the difference than to find the exact cause. With many choices you have to come to a decision based on imperfect information, which means making a decision before the landscape changes.

## CHOOSE THE MOMENT TO MAKE A CHOICE

All decisions are time bound, not just by deadlines but also because if you wait too long to decide, new developments will come along which change the territory. If you're deciding which new phone to buy, waiting for new models to come out means that you will never buy one. You have to decide to decide, and choosing when to make a decision is a key part of the process.

Many decision deadlines are, however, unreal. If you know that vital information is on its way to you, decide tomorrow. If you know most of what you need to know and your decision is required to move a process forward, make it and (see Strategy 2) unless you're proven to be painfully mistaken, stick to it.

## ACCEPT THAT 'GOOD ENOUGH' MAY HAVE TO DO

Ask people about big, important business decisions and they will often tell you that they can see how they might have made a different choice, but it wouldn't necessarily have been better. In our personal lives we tend not to use this approach, more often tempted by regret, sadness at the path not taken, or anger at others who blocked us doing things we wanted to do.

People who make good business decisions know that the vast majority of decisions are imperfect. They have to be, because they are made under time pressure with the (often incomplete) information that is available at the time.

Dig deeper into good business decision-making and you'll discover another principle: imperfect decision-making is the norm, but what happens next matters more than the decision. In other words, sticking to a decision, committing to it and making things happen, in many cases matters more than the original decision.

Clearly this doesn't apply if the decision is just plain wrong. Interestingly this is often when something is forced through a committee or on a majority vote when a significant number of people have already raised warning flags about implementation. Setting out to sea in the face of a gale warning is a dangerous game; acting blindly after clear warnings of negative consequences often betrays arrogance or a lack of imagination.

However, most sound decision-making operates on the 'good enough' benchmark: if the decision is 80–90% thought through it will be 80–90% right, and if it's 80–90% properly implemented it will work 80–90% of the time. Compare that to the product launches, rebranding exercises and organizational mergers that don't work, and you may conclude that 'good enough' is pretty good indeed.

# ADOPT THE 24-HOUR HABIT

If you're under stress or feeling vulnerable your decision-making powers go on the blink. So it's easy to be wrong-footed if something comes at you out of the blue. For example, you may just have had a difficult meeting with your boss, and you get a call from a recruitment agency. You might find yourself in a selection process without thinking.

Someone may ring or email making demands of you. Under stress it's much easier to have your guilt buttons pressed and to be bounced into doing something you won't enjoy and you don't have time for. It's equally possible for someone to flatter or cajole you into doing something you regret. Busy people often say 'yes' too easily; people under pressure say 'yes' or 'no' when they're not thinking at all, because their instincts are all about self-protection: making things go away.

The important point is that if you make these decisions on the hoof you won't recognize if they're important or not. When you're under pressure or feeling vulnerable, always try to give yourself 24 hours, even if what you're offered sounds brilliant. If it's vital to make a decision the same day, at least give yourself two hours, but in general 24 hours allows you to assess whether the step on offer makes sense, is achievable, and will be worth doing.

When you buy time, do so in the right tone of voice. Don't leave a caller feeling you're unsure or suspicious. It's far better to say 'that sounds fascinating – let me have a think'.

### Putting it all together

Do you have times which are good or bad for decision-making? Some people never decide anything before their second cup of coffee or when they're hungry; others know their judgement becomes rocky after 8 p.m. We're all subject to natural rhythms and perform better at certain times of day, and make worse decisions when we're tired or upset.

Recognize those moments of vulnerability when your critical powers go offline. Think of days you've said 'no' because you felt ill or grumpy, or 'yes' to please someone; or times you accepted dull projects because you felt nothing else would come along.

Taking time doesn't mean dithering or being a poor decision-maker, but allowing proper decision-making to take place. Considering a new role and a relocation, for example, might require thinking that takes place over several weeks and many conversations. Take long enough to know why you are saying yes or no. If you feel vulnerable or likely to make a decision you regret, buy some time, even if you are pretty of your. Few important requests need an immediate answer. Pause long enough to consider if there is a downside you haven't spotted, and what resources you'll need to be successful. On a day which exacts high pressure it's probably best not to make important life decisions. The day you fail an assessment is not a good day too be discussing the future of your marriage.

Don't over-interrogate past decisions, particularly those made under pressure. Stick to them, and live with 'good enough'.

## 13 Use problem solving more effectively

> 'We can't solve problems by using the same kind of thinking we used when we created them.' Albert Einstein

> 'A pessimist sees difficulty in every opportunity; an optimist sees opportunity in every difficulty.' Winston Churchill

> 'Creativity is allowing yourself to make mistakes. Art is knowing which ones to keep.' Scott Adams

> 'When we change the way we look at things, the things we look at change.' Wayne Dyer

> 'The greatest thing a human soul ever does in this world is to see something, and tell what it saw in a plain way. Hundreds of people can talk for one who can think, but thousands can think for one who can see. To see clearly is poetry, prophecy, and religion – all in one.' John Ruskin

The concept of *locus of control* was developed by Julian Rotter in the 1950s. It describes the way we explain experience by looking inside ourselves or outside at external factors. People with an *internal* locus of control tend to believe that their personal decisions have a big influence over life outcomes: individuals make their own success. They don't take setbacks personally or see them as part of a pattern. Those with an *external* locus of control believe that external forces, like luck, write the script. If they fail a driving test they blame the instructor, the road conditions, or fate.

It is argued that resilient people tend to have an internal locus of control – or that they choose to adopt one. A clear stage along the way is taking actions to make resourceful, realistic plans, combined with an improved approach to problem solving. Resilient behaviour is about planning ahead, and one way of doing that is to have plenty of tried and tested problem-solving tools at your fingertips.

One strategy people commonly use when something is on their mind is to write lists: 'to-do' lists, and lists of pros and cons. Both are helpful, up to a point. Action lists help you to 'park' activity: making a list last thing at night may allow you enough sense of control to turn the light off. Looking at pros and cons on paper may also clarify a problem.

Most planning is really organized worrying (see Chapter 10). You keep turning the problem around, looking at it from different angles, making lists. If you stay in one thinking mode for too long you get locked into it. Good planning requires problem-solving, and that requires forward movement: identifying the problem, analysing it, thinking up potential solutions, testing ideas out, and then allowing proper planning to take over at the implementation stage.

Problem solving assumes a goal – a solution. The belief that a solution can be found if enough time and imagination are applied to a problem is a fundamentally optimistic position. Human history also tells us that it generally works.

## REACH FOR YOUR EMERGENCY KIT

Under pressure you will forget random things: PINs, names, keyboard shortcuts. The emotionally overcharged brain plays strange tricks, including trying to kid you that you don't have any problem-solving ability. In these moments, objective tools help you think more clearly. Here's an emergency decision-making kit for use in white-knuckle moments:

### Diagnostics

- Do I really know what the problem is? Are there more facts to be gathered?
- Is the problem important? What happens if nothing changes?
- Is the problem urgent? When will things get worse?
- If I spoke to a trusted colleague, what would he/she see as the cause?
- What parts of the problem do I have any influence over?
- How much (or how little) information do I need to make a decision?

### Draft solution

- In broad terms, what would a solution look like? What might work?
- If that solution is unavailable, what else might work?
- What solutions have I used before? Do they really fit?
- What problems might the proposed solution create?

### Implementation

- What's the first step? What's the critical step?
- What resources do I need to allocate?
- How do I know if the solution is working? How do I know if I pull the plug too soon?
- How do I ensure I stick to the plan, even if I meet obstacles?
- What will tell me that the plan wasn't such a good idea?
- When do I review? How do I learn from this?

## PRACTISE WHEN THE HEAT IS OFF

Practise using your emergency kit on everyday problems. Psychologists often recommend that we improve problem-solving strategies by using them more thoroughly when dealing with ordinary, low-impact crises.

Look back at the kind of problem that has previously made you feel frozen like a rabbit in the headlights, unable to move, unable to think. When you did manage to think, you felt like you were in a fog. If you thought of solutions, they seemed glib or wildly optimistic.

If you recognize the times when you are paralysed by indecision, train yourself to adopt a more methodical approach when dealing with routine problems. In fact, taking a moment to review rather than getting stuck in every time will generally improve your problem-solving skills, provide better analysis, and prevent knee-jerk reactions (jumping at the quickest, most obvious solution) or historic reactions ('this looks like the kind of problem I've solved in the past, so I will apply an off-the-shelf solution').

## STEP BACK FROM THE PROBLEM

Stepping back from the problem is also a good idea, because it allows you to reframe it, and because you start to take yourself out of the situation. One obvious method is to talk to someone else about the problem. They may interpret the facts very differently. An objective friend will also listen to your language to check if (1) you understand the problem or if you are just reacting to it and (2) to see if you are catastrophizing (see Chapter 42). This often works best with someone who is not closely involved in your work context, and you definitely get better results by talking to someone who is not part of the problem or affected by the solution.

Other ways of stepping back from the problem include:

- Testing yourself: is there really a problem?
- Allowing time to do its job: how likely is it that the problem will solve itself or go away?
- Imagining that you were someone you admire facing the same problem.
- Using lateral thinking: in what ways is this problem like apparently unrelated things you have done elsewhere?
- Playing 'what if?' games : e.g. 'what if nothing changes?' 'What if all my solutions were barred?'
- Trying draft or test solutions and pilot schemes.
- Building on experience by asking for previously implemented answers: don't assume you're the first person to fix this.
- Don't patch up something that needs serious renovation.
- On the other hand, don't be afraid of swift fixes. 'Quick and dirty' can sometimes be 'swift and elegant'.
- Don't overrate independence. Ask for help.

## Putting it all together

You might assume that decision-making is about logical thinking. Some of it is, particularly where you have to take a step-by-step approach. Start by deconstructing the issue enough to spot tentative solutions.

However, many important decisions are not about logic at all. For example, deciding whether you will fit into an organizational culture or whether you trust someone enough to go into partnership is about decoding non-logical information. If you find yourself talking about 'gut feeling', don't assume that's a secondary or less reliable source of information. Some things just 'feel' right, and our judgement is accurate. Bold and brilliant decisions are made on exactly this basis – largely because we invest more energy and commitment in things we trust. Instinctively you may be choosing to go with the grain of a situation (see Chapter 41), using gut feeling to match yourself to an opportunity.

A key factor in resilience is taking decisive actions in adverse situations. One way to do that is to have some kind of strategy in mind – a pre-prepared emergency kit for overwhelming problems. Planning ahead is also about anticipating how you might be thrown off-balance by predictable events, and how you might begin to react to the unpredictable. Look hard at what happens to your decision-making, planning and problem-solving skills when you find yourself in the hot seat. Trying out and improving problem-solving skills before that day comes along is a great defence strategy. It also stops your overcharged brain robbing you of confidence that you can solve problems.

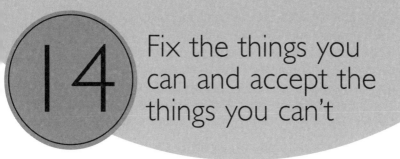

# 14

# Fix the things you can and accept the things you can't

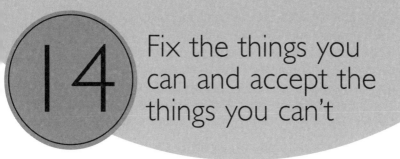

> 'For every ailment under the sun
> There is a remedy, or there is none;
> If there be one, try to find it;
> If there be none, never mind it.' Anon.

> 'God, grant me the serenity to accept the things I cannot change, the courage to change the things I can, and wisdom to know the difference.' Serenity Prayer, attributed to Reinhold Niebuhr

> 'A person will sometimes devote all his life to the development of one part of his body – the wishbone.' Robert Frost

> 'When you have to make a choice and don't make it, that is in itself a choice.' William James

> 'When one door closes, another opens; but we often look so long and so regretfully upon the closed door that we do not see the one which has opened for us.' Alexander Graham Bell

If you worry about getting everything done, think about the consequences; the better you perform, the more new tasks you'll be given. You can go from star performer to swamped in a month. In today's workplace it's common to be required to do the work of more than one employee, and multi-tasking and priority juggling are fairly routine.

How you deal with this is one of the hallmarks of a resilient professional life. Trying to complete an ever-lengthening, ever more complex list of tasks is a recipe for burn-out, and as soon as a stressed state becomes an anxiety state, your judgement starts to become less reliable (see Chapter 9). Soon you don't see the wood from the trees and everything seems equally urgent. Ironically, these moments where people overwork with diminishing results are also times when people are seen as under-performing, even if in fact they are working harder than everyone else. The reason is they are not working hardest – or visibly – on things that matter to the organization (see Chapter 28).

Working wisdom is often about discernment – the ability to adopt a quieter state of mind or to teach yourself how to judge things carefully – and sometimes this simply means working a little more slowly. Discernment allows additional objectivity, often gained from insights into what really matters. If you want to protect yourself from undue work stress, it helps to be able to discern the difference between the things you have some control over and the things you don't.

This is powerful stuff. Things you have no control over can often be left alone. Sometimes there's no point worrying about them until you have new information, a decision, or until things move along to the point where you can add something usefully. Things you have no control over at all must wait, in fact, because early tinkering will be wasted effort.

Be scrupulous in your attention to the things you can fix, even just a little – in other words, the things where a small amount of input from you can move something forward.

## LOOK FOR QUICK WINS

Having decided on the things you really can fix, it's important to think about timescales. Some solutions will take longer to implement than others. For example, restructuring an organization or changing its culture, or designing a new product or method, can take years. Your work might impact on success, but only if you get a result that is on time, on cost (and is what the organization still needs when it's implemented).

Working towards long-term results does little to help when you're expected to deliver immediately, so shorten the timescale by looking for quick wins. If you've just moved into a new job quick wins can be easy to spot. Some are obvious opportunities for you to do things you have done before, where you can get swift results in return for minimal effort. The classic quick win is often described as 'low on cost and high on imagination'.

Another type of opportunity is often described as 'picking low-hanging fruit'. Work colleagues are often clear about opportunities that are being missed or things that regularly get in the way of productivity. By listening and responding you might be able to come up with a smart solution, especially if it draws on your experience. Do, however, be careful to acknowledge that the idea is not your own.

## HOW TO IGNORE THE THINGS THAT DON'T MATTER MUCH

You may notice that your colleagues have a wide range of strategies for ignoring tasks and deadlines, but only if they can get away with it without pain. Indeed, one way of judging the importance of a task is to ask yourself if anyone will notice if it remains uncompleted, and if it is noticed, what are the consequences? We're all a little bit driven by pain, blame and shame; no-one likes having the finger pointed at them because they let the side down.

There will always come a point when some tasks on your desk don't get completed. How do you ignore them? One strategy is to touch them lightly so they move along: one comment, one signature, one helpful suggestion and pass the problem along. Others will and must fall into the category of 'doesn't matter, and probably never will'.

Sometimes the best way of ignoring tasks is by testing them – leave them alone for a week or two and see what happens. One headmaster of my acquaintance used to put every incoming letter from his local authority straight into the bin. 'If it really matters they'll ring me and ask for something', he said. For most of us, having a file marked 'Work in Progress' which we secretly label 'Stuff I Am Going To Ignore' will do the trick – but do watch out for issues where your judgement is wrong and a failure to respond gets red flagged. If in doubt, check with colleagues on how incoming tasks should be prioritized, both in terms of irritation quotient and of how much you put yourself at risk if you fail to comply.

# DEALING WITH AN OVERLOADED 'TO-DO' LIST

It's easy to develop an ever-expanding 'to do' list. Some people revel in them, waving these lists about to show how busy and important they are.

An extensive 'to-do' list with big, chunky items on it can feel like something heavy you carry round with you all day, and can diminish your resilience. (See Chapter 25 on asking for help). Feeling you have little control over the task, and less control over what comes in next, adds to your stress.

Look at your task list again and ask yourself what is important, what is urgent, and – fundamentally – what really matters. We're not talking about the meaning of the universe here, but doing what professionals do every day, discerning what is urgent and what is important, and moving quickest on things which fit both categories. Some of the important items are likely to push your ratings up at work. Other actions may help you avoid disaster.

Another way of looking at your list is to decide how much of it is really down to you. Some items are really SEPs, my shorthand for Someone Else's Problem.

### Putting it all together

Under pressure you may feel that you're trying to hold back a tide of information requests and conflicting deadlines. The danger with working in an overload state is that you only see how busy you are and how stressed you feel, and you don't take time out to ask two important questions: (1) 'how much of this matters?' and (2) 'am I missing the things that do matter?'.

Gain perspective by remembering that many organizations issue requests for reports that will never be read, and require immediate responses for non-urgent matters. Organizations love to collect information, but the amount of data required is often over-specified. What's even more worrying is that after busy people have scurried around finding numbers to add to the latest statistical analysis, the resulting reports may never be read and acted upon. Much of work is unproductive tail-chasing.

Organizations love to invent data management processes, and sometimes invent so many that fulfilling their exact requirements would occupy more than 24 hours a day. This means that what you're really doing is learning to decode incoming demands and find out what will make a difference – both to the organization and to your reputation.

Focus on the things you can fix, or at least make a contribution to. Look hard at the things you can't influence. If they matter, find the tools or support you need so you can play your part. If they don't matter, look hard at the idea of deflecting or ignoring them.

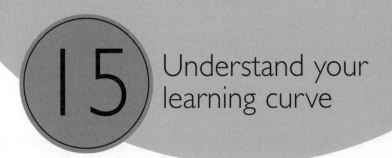

# 15 Understand your learning curve

> 'A learning experience is one of those things that say, "You know that thing you just did? Don't do that."' Douglas Adams

> 'We learn by example and by direct experience because there are real limits to the adequacy of verbal instruction.' Malcolm Gladwell

> 'One of the reasons people stop learning is that they become less and less willing to risk failure.' John W. Gardner

> 'The illiterate of the twenty-first century will not be those who cannot read and write, but those who cannot learn, unlearn, and relearn.' Alvin Toffler

> 'We learn geology the morning after the earthquake.' Ralph Waldo Emerson

Every job can be described in terms of a learning curve which stretches from your first to last day in a role. The first few weeks in a job are often stimulating, simply because you're learning about a new organization. If you're saying that the learning curve is steep, that's a positive sign: you're making progress, even if it feels like a white-knuckle ride.

Learning the job quickly and without fuss is a fundamental requirement in most roles. However, it exposes workers to elevated stress levels – partly because of the impact of learning things and proving yourself under pressure, and partly because it means exposing vulnerability – in learning mode you are more dependent and less secure. In a time when you weren't let loose until you were trained, you could make mistakes in a safe environment; today you're expected to avoid critical mistakes but at the same time learn things as quickly as possible.

Eventually, even in complex roles, the curve flattens out. This may take just two to three months, or it may take a couple of annual cycles. Roles such as sales and recruitment are classic examples of jobs which are highly stimulating for a year or two and then can become repetitive processes.

What happens when the learning curve flattens out? If you're not given opportunities to learn new things, it's likely that you'll start to feel under-stretched and under-challenged. The net result is that your motivation starts to decline. If you feel that you are not being challenged, it's easy to start feeling that you are not making a strong contribution any more. A flattened learning curve quickly diminishes your resilience. Some people start to doubt their own worth, others all into the trap of looking and sounding jaded and cynical. Where people feel underemployed and under-challenged this is picked up by others. This issue is of course magnified where the economic climate encourages workers to sit tight in a job rather than allowing market pressures to move them on.

## DON'T HANG ABOUT

When you take on a new role or project, how quickly do you get on top of things?

Two generations ago you would only be allowed to undertake a new role once you had received weeks, if not months, of training. This might involve classroom training, observing and working alongside someone else as a trainee, and then only beginning the role when you had demonstrated the ability to use skills unsupervised.

In today's economy employers expect new hires to 'hit the deck running'. If you haven't already got the skills, you need to pick them up pretty fast. You probably won't get any formal training and only light supervision. You'll be expected to pick up the underlying product and organizational knowledge pretty fast, possibly in your own time.

Learn as quickly as you can, using the learning method that suits you best. If you don't know where to begin, observe others around you in terms of what they do to get on top of things quickly. Keep asking for short cuts – methods of getting from A to Z rapidly.

## BE UPFRONT ABOUT YOUR LEARNING STRENGTHS

A generation ago it was fine for some parts of the workforce to be upfront about their reluctance (or refusal) to learn new skills or technologies. As the speed of change accelerates, such an attitude quickly communicates lack of employability. Saying you don't have time or motivation to learn is a career-limiting statement. Saying you struggle to learn is heard as saying you can't. Worse still, if you start to believe this yourself you undermine yourself, and you are certainly less resilient, simply because you are starting to let go of the tools that will help you survive the next wave.

Most organizations now explicitly require fast learners. Showing how and where you have demonstrated this ability is often a great way of emphasizing your usefulness. Show how you can pick up a new topic quickly and hit the deck running. Give examples of where you have acquired new skills under pressure.

That's all very well if you're a fast learner, but not everyone fits that category. Others need more time to process information, reflect, and try things out for themselves. That's fine in most contexts, as long as you manage this learning style and make it fit. So don't claim to be fully informed if you haven't got there yet, and don't express blasé confidence in your own skills if they need adjusting. Instead, negotiate the time and support you need, or just take a little more time. Saying something like 'I'm pretty much on top of this, but I need to go away and work it through a couple of times' shows the right mix of commitment and self-awareness. However you learn, get up to your maximum speed in the way you know best.

# NEGOTIATE A JOB REFIT

How quickly do you get bored with a job? When does boredom start to eat away at your resilience?

If your role no longer stimulates you, don't follow the herd by throwing yourself at the job market. You'll probably be offered a role similar to your present one. The first few months may be stimulating because the environment is novel and you'll have to learn about new products and systems, but if the job is fundamentally a repeat of your last one, you're back to square one. It's always better to try to fix the job you're in than to seek a new one for the wrong reasons.

Job negotiation begins by undertaking an honest audit about what you've contributed in the last 12 months, but in this case also focus on what you have learned. Next, identify a way of changing the shape of your job. This might be a project, pilot scheme, secondment, attachment to another team, or swapping some responsibilities for others. Present the idea with enthusiasm rather than as a complaint about your current role. The phrase 'this is how you can get really good value out of me' may help; make sure you offer something which is a clear win-win, refreshing your role but also clearly adding value to the organization.

## Putting it all together

If you move into a new role you're aware of your learning curve. Responsiveness to training is partly about speed of assimilation, but it's also about enthusiasm. Demonstrating a hunger for new information and new ways of working is a great way to build an industry reputation. It also feeds resilience – you are constantly restocking your toolkit to provide resources to help you when challenges come along.

Learning curves rarely remain flat – they dip. When they do, it's not just your brain that feels the effect; engagement begins to tail. Look at past experiences to identify the point a job started to feel repetitive and no longer offered new learning. How did that affect your work performance and motivation levels? What did you do to change things?

Astute organizations recognize that learning curves can be pushed above the horizontal. The right mix is dependent on the individual, but the answer is nearly always about a challenge that takes the individual beyond their comfort zone; this might be about a new project or a learning event, but might just as easily be an opportunity to mentor or train others.

Our economy provides little space or time for organizations to manage learning beyond the initial induction period – negotiating the rest is largely up to you. Learning to renegotiate and shape your role so that it's a better fit is a great start. Give equal attention to your reputation; be careful not to send out messages that suggest a reluctance to learn.

# 16  Learn from others

❝ *'In everyone's life, at some time, our inner fire goes out. It is then burst into flame by an encounter with another human being. We should all be thankful for those people who rekindle the inner spirit.'* Albert Schweitzer

❝ *'Remember, if you ever need a helping hand, it's at the end of your arm; as you get older, remember you have another hand. The first is to help yourself, the second is to help others.'* Audrey Hepburn

❝ *'We awaken in others the same attitude of mind we hold toward them.'* Elbert Hubbard

❝ *'There is nothing new under the sun but there are lots of old things we don't know.'* Ambrose Bierce

❝ *'Knowledge becomes wisdom only after it has been put to good use.'* Mark Twain

It's surprising how many people say they have stopped learning at work. Sometimes it's because they have reached a point on their learning curve where they're not being stretched any more (see Chapter 15). If they are really not learning anything at all (and that could simply be the self-justification statement of a closed mind), it's probably because they're ignoring a resource which is very close by.

There's an old training term you don't hear often today. It referred to a method called 'sitting next to Nellie'. This describes one of the simplest and oldest forms of on-the-job training: sitting next to someone who is doing the job and learning by watching, copying, trying things out for yourself, and getting immediate feedback from someone who knows what they're doing.

Modern learning and development professionals don't use the term 'sitting next to Nellie' because it's archaic and sexist, but it wasn't such a bad learning method. Watching what people do provides fairly reliable information about timings, processes and skills. We also absorb something of the best working style to adopt to be productive and safe. Ironically, although the training model was directive, it was a method which required workers to listen, observe attentively, and then put behaviours into practice under supervision.

Today Nellie has been replaced by a handbook or, more likely, an Intranet learning programme, a phone App, or a YouTube video. The problem about this kind of self-directed learning is that Nellie taught us far more than a set of skills. Sitting down with a skilled professional also teaches us a mindset, an attitude to work. You learned as much from the way Nellie interacted with her supervisor as you did from watching her hands.

People watching is the most hard-wired kind of learning. You can learn by directly asking people how they do something, perhaps getting a mini-demonstration. You can learn indirectly by observing behaviours and then putting them into practice in your own style. This works best if you can get some objective feedback about your work performance, along with encouragement to try additional strategies.

## NOTICE WALKING TEXTBOOKS

Closely observing others is a great way of learning, as long as you attend properly to what they are doing. The first step is to value skills you don't see as important. You might notice, for example, how some people can delegate huge tasks diplomatically, or how another person quietly resolves conflict in a meeting.

The workplace is full of walking textbooks – people who can teach you something simply by working next to you, or at least close by. That assumes, of course, that you are prepared to look, and take the time to do so.

Listening to other people at work teaches you a huge amount, too. Tone and phrasing makes the difference between an idea which might fly and one that will go down like a lead balloon. Listen to what people say and how they say it, particularly where they have to communicate something difficult. If you find someone who appears to be a good communicator, seek opportunities to watch them in different contexts. Allow yourself some surprises – some individuals are poor at one-to-one exchanges but great performers in front of an audience, and vice versa.

## LEARN THROUGH OTHERS AS WELL AS FROM THEM

Just because you're reading this book on your own doesn't mean you should use it on your own. Look at the topics raised, particularly the ones which make you feel uncomfortable. Try out some of the strategies. When you have done so, share your thinking with someone else. One of the best ways of learning from others is to try things out for yourself and then review your results, your learning, and the problems you experienced with someone else.

This is even more valuable where you try out soft skills, particularly in complex situations. For example you might want to improve your ability at networking. As soon as you do so you will probably recognize that the learning pathway is complicated. You have to think about your objectives, decode social and business situations, learn how to communicate effectively and naturally, and how to open doors for yourself without appearing pushy or fake.

Trying to learn all that purely by deduction or by teaching yourself is close to impossible. Observe how others do it, try it out for yourself, and find someone to help you unpack the experience. A good coach won't allow you to simply announce success or failure, but will draw out from you what went well, what didn't, and what you can do differently next time. Reflection is a powerful learning tool, but often someone else needs to be your mirror.

## LEARN COLLABORATIVELY

Just because our work culture expects you to organize your own learning doesn't mean this is the best or only method of personal development.

Collaborative learning is a method of learning alongside others, sharing insights into the way you learn as well as information. There is a wealth of educational research evidence that collaborative learning groups achieve higher levels of thought and retain information longer than students who learn alone. Shared learning helps students engage in discussion, take responsibility for their own learning, and become critical thinkers. Often groups focus on a common problem or mutual goal. A common feature is that individuals go away to absorb information on their own and then share their learning with others.

Collaborative learning also means that you are accountable to each other for your learning activity. Typically learners in such groups talk openly about where they find learning difficult. They gain support from others with very different learning styles and learn new strategies. For example, some learn by debate and discussion while others are much better at reading and synthesizing text. Some of us absorb theory, others need to try things in practice.

Investigate online collaborative learning. Modern communication technology allows groups to operate where individuals are geographically disperse, using live online discussions, LinkedIn groups or discussion threads to explore ideas. You can work with people in one organization, one sector, or explore exciting multi-disciplinary and international possibilities. Leading and regularly contributing to discussions in online groups can be a great way of opening up learning conversations and tracking down people with important knowledge and experience.

## Putting it all together

We live in an individualistic and self-reliant culture. In recent years organizations have cut back on training budgets, so increasingly our learning happens in isolation, through books or screens, or simply by working things out for ourselves.

Your workplace (or your clients and contacts if you work outside an organization) provide some of the richest material when you are learning and developing interpersonal skills. However you only learn if you watch and listen properly. This means attending to the full range of things people do – words chosen, tone, body language, timing, context, style. Sometimes that means putting aside your preconceptions about what is and isn't a good working manner. Develop a fascination for the way people exercise even the most modest skills.

The richest learning comes from quietly observing people under pressure. If your relationship with your role model makes it appropriate, pass on positive feedback. People generally have a sense of what they do well, but not always why. Observe, then absorb. Try approaches out. Use the borrowed phrases now and again – but not so much you look like a clone or sound like a parrot. Although imitation is the sincerest form of flattery, make sure when you 'borrow' behaviours or language that what you do avoids looking like mimicry.

It's unethical to steal ideas, but great to build on other people's values, behaviours and strategies. Don't just choose role models in the world of celebrities and movie stars. Strong professionals learn from just about anyone around them.

# Recognize how far other people impact on your resilience

> **"** 'O, wad some Power the giftie gie us
> To see oursels as others see us!' Robert Burns

> **"** 'Criticism may not be agreeable, but it is necessary. It fulfils
> the same function as pain in the human body. It calls
> attention to an unhealthy state of things.' Winston Churchill

> **"** 'A man can fail many times, but he isn't a failure until he
> begins to blame somebody else.' John Burroughs

> **"** 'Remember: when people tell you something's wrong or doesn't
> work for them, they are almost always right. When they tell
> you exactly what they think is wrong and how to fix it, they
> are almost always wrong.' Neil Gaiman

> **"** 'Our chief want is someone who will inspire us to be what we
> know we could be.' Ralph Waldo Emerson

Resilience is often tested by circumstances, but there's usually a people dimension. Colleagues at work help you to get things done, but they can also play an important role in pushing you up or down the work satisfaction scale. If you are even moderately thin-skinned your self-esteem may be elevated by praise and flattened by criticism, sometimes within a ten-minute time slot.

Think about how your resilience has been strengthened or weakened by those around you, particularly in terms of feedback. You may have been fortunate to have a manager who actively encouraged you to develop yourself. You may have worked with others who have equally effectively got in your way or dragged you back. Some co-workers instinctively support, showing you the ropes when you begin and passing on useful information. Others actively play a more political game of withholding information and setting traps. Some simply ignore you. In a competitive environment you may be set up to fail.

Managers have a large impact on an individual's confidence and development. A 2005 Chartered Institute of Personnel & Development (CIPD) survey on the way HR practitioners plan their careers indicated that 50% of them considered their line manager as the most influential source of career advice. You can turn that on its head and imagine the damage that is done if that manager fails to give good advice or actively blocks your way forward. Your first boss often has a huge impact in terms of the way you picture yourself in work, and the strategies you use when working. My first boss, for example, told me that 'if you've got something difficult to say, don't put it in writing', wise advice which has prevented no end of trouble.

Look back on the way past managers have encouraged you or diminished you. How many encouraged you to begin to take control yourself? Enlightened managers teach their staff to be independent learners. Are you still reliant on your boss to lift your spirits, pat you on the back, and patch you up when you fall? Isn't it time you did a little more of that for yourself?

## WATCH THE TRAFFIC LIGHTS

Reflect on times when you have needed encouragement and feedback and didn't get it. Perhaps you didn't know how to ask, or you didn't have the confidence to do so. Alternatively you may have been seeking constructive feedback from the wrong person at the wrong time.

When you feel dependent on encouragement to keep your performance on track, seek out natural allies. However if you can only move forward based on feedback from particular individuals, for example your manager, learn to read the signals better. Think of them in terms of green, amber and red:

Green – You're picking up a lot of positive and encouraging messages. It's OK to ask for specific feedback on how you're doing (but not too often).

Amber – You're getting mixed signals. You're probably only going to get feedback at the end of the task, if you do it well. Don't seek too much feedback until you have delivered.

Red – You're going to get either zero feedback or a response which may appear cold, even hostile. Get the job done, and seek feedback outside the process.

If you have any choice about the people you work with, do everything you can to go for green. People who give supportive and meaningful feedback help you build up a reservoir of self-confidence, and indirectly steer you towards experiences and skills which are seen as useful by your organization.

## DO WHAT YOU CAN TO AVOID BEING SET UP TO FAIL

Jean-François Manzoni and Jean-Louis Barsoux came up with *The Set-Up-To-Fail Syndrome* (Harvard Business School Press, 2002). The theory provides insights into what happens when you work for a new boss. The idea is that managers form a strong impression about your usefulness very quickly, after seeing you in action just once or twice. Research reveals that managers decide early whether you are a future star performer, or someone not worth investing in. What happens next is that managers give interesting tasks and positive feedback to the stars, and (often unconsciously) set others up to fail . The non-stars are given work where it is less easy to succeed and shine. Managers unconsciously undermine the performance of staff through ineffective feedback and weak interventions, or sometimes by actively putting them in situations where failure is inevitable. A very simple example is where a manager constantly delegates to your weaknesses (so you continue to under-perform) rather than to your strengths.

Your boss's first impression and initial judgements about whether you're a natural winner or loser is instinctive and based on the first few occasions you are noticed. This means that you need to be very clear when beginning a role (or when your boss changes – see below) to send out signals which indicate focus, competence and enthusiasm.

## NEW BOSS, NEW IMPACT

Changes of senior staff are frequent. If you find yourself with a new boss you have an important and rare opportunity to re-set the reputation clock. Your boss hasn't worked with you before. He or she may have had a quick verbal summary of your strengths and weaknesses from colleagues, but since your boss is overwhelmed with data right now, this information is only half-absorbed. You have an important opportunity to reveal yourself in a new light.

Refresh your impact. Sharpen up your image: consider buying some new work outfits. Put real effort into looking and sounding energetic and on the ball. If you help your new boss to settle in you will make an impression fast.

This new boss is likely to want an overview of your role and how it fits in, so prepare to communicate that in language which conveys enthusiasm, talking about how you contribute to the big picture (see Chapter 43). Show an interest in your new boss's experience and ideas. Go out of your way to be helpful in these initial meetings, making it clear that you're a great information resource and happy to make your boss's life easier. As you get to know this new decision-maker in your life, recommend short cuts that will make your boss look good. Then start to negotiate opportunities to do more of the things you do well.

### Putting it all together

A minority of workers are happy to operate alone; others feed on human interaction. Supportive people make a difference to our long-term resilience. Positive strokes aren't nice bonuses added to a working day; they enable you to bank up confidence like a kind of psychological buffer offering some protection against future knock-backs. Sustained praise and feedback improve your mood and impact on your behaviours, but the feedback does of course need to be meaningful.

It's obvious that key decision-makers in your organization have a major impact on your future. These are the people who decide how much responsibility you should take on, which projects you join, whether you get promoted or transferred. Even after you have left an organization they can still influence your future through informal references. If your contribution is noticed and valued, there's a greater chance that development opportunities will follow. Therefore it follows that the impact of your work is dependent on others, and so in turn is your resilience.

Talk to workers who have reached the top levels in organizations and they will usually point to a combination of internal and external factors. They took control of their own progress, but they also took active steps to do two other things: they sought out supporters, champions and mentors (mentors can play a vital part in helping you decode an organization and improve the way you fit into it), and they actively decided when to influence and impress key decision-makers.

# 18 Believe in yourself just a little more

> 'If you have made mistakes, there is always another chance for you. You may have a fresh start any moment you choose, for this thing we call "failure" is not the falling down, but the staying down.' Mary Pickford

> 'There are two ways to slide easily through life: to believe everything or to doubt everything; both ways save us from thinking.' Alfred Korbzybski

> 'You can't connect the dots looking forward; you can only connect them looking backwards. So you have to trust that the dots will somehow connect in your future. You have to trust in something – your gut, destiny, life, karma, whatever. This approach has never let me down, and it has made all the difference in my life.' Steve Jobs

> 'Whatever you believe with feeling becomes your reality.' Brian Tracy

> 'We must not, in trying to think about how we can make a big difference, ignore the small daily differences we can make which, over time, add up to big differences that we often cannot foresee.' Mariam Wright

You expected to see self-belief discussed, didn't you? And now you're thinking about skipping this chapter. Before you do, note its title says *just a little more*.

The problem with a great deal of literature on self-belief is that it's written in absolute terms. Mistrust advice that seems to suggest that all you do is flick a switch to solve all self-doubt, or if you verbalize one phrase with utter certainty you can conquer the world. When you're worried about a meeting or a presentation it doesn't really help when someone says 'act naturally'. Again, this situation isn't about an on/off state. It's about gradual forward movement rather than remaining stuck.

The reason motivational speakers take a black-and-white approach is that often we really do need a push, an injection of energy, to shake us out of one state into another. Sometimes saying 'knock 'em dead' to someone just before they make a speech really does elevate their performance. Anyone or anything that provides you with a little more enthusiastic commitment is to be seized with both hands. However the 'believe in yourself and you can do anything' approach fails to reveal that self-belief is about growth and development; although small acorns can grow to be mighty oaks, time and nurturing also plays a vital part.

Self-belief makes a really important contribution to resilience. Choosing to believe that you can do something is a powerful antidote to the lethargy and resistance that prevents you from making a change.

State (yes, say it out loud) your belief that you can make things happen in your life. It's the first step in doing something different, something creative. Hold on to it, at least for a short time. This might be simply about rethinking where you are or beginning to manage your feelings. Ultimately it's a two-stage decision: (1) you can make a difference to your situation in small steps, and (2) the first small step is to believe that you can make a difference to yourself or the circumstances around you.

## STEP ACROSS THE DOTTED LINE

Imagine you are standing in a large space with your toes against a dotted white line.

On this side of the line you believe your negative thoughts. You accept that how you see things now is the way you will always see them. You feel you know how others see you, and it's unimpressive. You have decided that you have no control over your feelings and where they take you. You are firmly convinced that there are no options available.

The other side of the dotted line comes from your memory of who you are on a good day. Think of real moments; remember what you were like. Remember how you felt, how things looked.

Now give yourself the good news. You don't need to change everything to cross the dotted line, to reconnect with your more productive self. You don't have to resolve every problem, deal with every uncertainty. You only need to choose to do one thing – take a single step over the line. This may be a decision to worry about something later, or to act on part of a problem. It might be about trusting your instincts to say 'no' or 'yes'.

When we think of difficult changes we imagine a long, hard climb up a mountain. We think of how much pain there will be in the last few paces taking us to the summit. The important question isn't what stops you from reaching the top of the mountain but what prevents you putting one foot forward and taking that first step. One step only. You don't have to complete the whole journey. Don't worry too much if you take a backward step; that happens too.

Remember that first step is probably not about you working alone, writing lists or looking things up on the internet. It's probably a face-to-face conversation with someone helpful who cares about you.

## SEE RESULTS AS TEMPORARY

The way we interpret events is often instinct dressed up as reasoning, so we invent absolutes. We say 'I've failed', rather than 'that strategy didn't work'. We tend to see setbacks as permanent. Perhaps that doesn't really mean 'forever', but it might as well as far as your mindset is concerned.

Most setbacks are temporary, and most errors are quickly forgotten. You may think something is hanging over your head forever, but usually colleagues have new concerns. People who are optimistic (or choose to be so) see events as temporary. It's a Western version of the Buddhist principle that everything experienced is 'passing', something we should not hang onto.

Watch out for the way you mis-label temporary troubles. For instance, next time you hear yourself say something like 'my views are always ignored at team meetings', start the sentence again so that it is a true snapshot of where things are right now: 'today my opinion wasn't acted upon'. The rest is about reflecting on the experience in a way that helps you change something. Were you clear enough? Were you talking so much that it was missed? Did you make it clear that what you were saying felt important to you? If you're uncertain of any of the answers, ask for honest feedback from a supportive team member.

## RUN THE RIGHT KIND OF MOVIE

There's a theory in sport science that visualizing activity is as powerful as the experienced event. It's claimed that a strong visualization of an action imprints itself on your brain as powerfully as the memory of an actual experience. Athletes are therefore encouraged to work hard at imagining how it feels to clear the bar or beat their best time.

Try it for yourself. For example, if you have to speak in public, picture yourself finishing your talk with the audience highly attentive and on your side. Visualize each detail: how you're standing, how your voice sounds, the speed and volume of your words, your eye contact with the audience. When that picture is strong and clear, run it repeatedly. Give yourself a visual reminder (such as a large coloured star on the side of your notes) which will reconnect you with that internal movie during the event.

**Putting it all together**

Some people are able to maintain a rock-like certainty about their abilities (this may be less rock-like than you believe: see Chapter 19 on Imposter Syndrome). Self-belief is like an outfit: sometimes worn with pride, but half the time left to gather moths.

American psychologist Suzanne Kobasa believes that resilient people view a difficulty as a challenge, not a paralysing event. They look at mistakes as opportunities for growth. Kobasa maintains that resilient people are committed to their lives and their goals, to relationships, the causes they care about, and their religious or spiritual beliefs.

To say such an approach is about mindset is to trivialize one of the most important choices we can make, which is to choose to commit – not just to action, but to believing in yourself enough so that you are enabled to make change possible. This matters most when you feel lost, helpless, or powerless to take action.

Clearly it's easy to believe in yourself when things are going brilliantly. The hard task is believing in yourself when things are going against you. It is work: you have to put in effort to swim against the tide of your own feelings. Otherwise, just going along with your mood means accepting as true any version of yourself that comes to mind.

Practise running great high-definition videos of yourself doing important things you find hard to do. The brain is a strange object: you can even learn from things you have never done before.

# 19 Deal with Imposter Syndrome

> 'Each time I write a book, every time I face that yellow pad, the challenge is so great. I have written eleven books, but each time I think, "Uh oh, they're going to find out now. I've run a game on everybody and they're going to find me out."'
> Maya Angelou

> 'The fundamental cause of the trouble is that in the modern world the stupid are cocksure while the intelligent are full of doubt.' Bertrand Russell

> 'One of the things I learned the hard way was that it doesn't pay to get discouraged. Keeping busy and making optimism a way of life can restore your faith in yourself.' Lucille Ball

> 'He may look like an idiot and talk like an idiot but don't let that fool you. He really is an idiot.' Groucho Marx

> 'The secret of life is honesty and fair dealing. If you can fake that, you've got it made.' Groucho Marx

Do you feel a fraud at work? It's a common feeling. Many executives reveal privately that a great deal of the time they feel their work is all pretence. Typically they say: 'I feel as if I got my job because I was lucky and that people don't notice that I am not qualified for it. I half expect someone to come along out of the blue one day and say, "OK, we know you're a fake. Empty your desk, leave today, and nothing more will be said." If someone said that I would probably just leave.'

The striking thing about Imposter Syndrome, first identified in the 1970s, is how many people feel they are a phoney – a fake – despite overwhelming evidence of their competence. They are the imposter who has taken the place of someone who really knows how to do the job. This is experienced by many very senior people who, in some circumstances, dismiss any of their achievements as mere luck, chance timing, the influence of others, or even a clerical error ('I don't think they meant to short-list me'). They believe they have somehow managed to hold their office through an undetected error, and it's just a matter of time before they're found out.

Writing in *The Guardian* in November 2013, Oliver Burkeman wrote 'it's a classic case of "comparing your insides with other people's outsides": you have access only to your own self-doubt, so you mistakenly conclude it's more justified than anyone else's'.

These are not simply self-defeating inner conversations. They affect how people see their abilities and decide which opportunities are within their scope. Burkeman refers to the work of US sociologists Jessica Collett and Jade Avelis, who wanted to know why female academics who aim for high-status academic positions 'downshift' towards something less ambitious. A survey of 460 doctoral students revealed that this was not about lifestyle choice but confidence, particularly among women: Collett stated in *Science* in September 2013 that 'Imposterism is something that negatively affects both men and women, but it's more pronounced among women, and therefore affects their career trajectories more.'

## NAME IT AND SHAME IT

What can you do to combat the feeling that you're an undiscovered fake? The danger is not just an edgy feeling that you're not quite good enough, but something which is close to a sense of shame. This isn't just a privately held doubt; it can prevent you from putting yourself forward for interesting roles or projects.

Start by naming what you feel. You're not the first to experience Imposter Syndrome. There will be others in your organization who also experience it (see below). Recognize that the feeling is perfectly normal, and learn to smile at the enormous creativity you put into trashing your own confidence.

Secondly, put it into context. Imposterism creeps in where you are isolated. People who perform the same kinds of task as other team members don't feel a fake so much because they receive fairly constant feedback that their contribution is up to standard. As soon as you take on more responsible and more lonely roles such feedback becomes thin on the ground. Ironically this is because what others generally see is a self-contained, confident exterior – they assume you don't need encouragement and won't take kindly to criticism. Those at or close to the very top of organizations often have no one around to tell them they are doing a good job, or to steer them towards more constructive behaviours.

If you work with a mentor, find someone you can openly discuss this problem with. If you believe that disclosing this area of self-doubt makes you appear weak, you haven't yet found someone you can trust enough. Recruit supporters (see Chapter 38) who will actively remind you of your tangible achievements.

## LOOK UPWARDS

The revealing thing about the Imposter Syndrome is that we believe that the staff above us in organizations are immune from it. Imposterism is of course rarely revealed except to trusted colleagues, and the rest of the world sees a confident, unshakeable self, so it's unlikely that you would notice the syndrome in senior colleagues.

So, two worlds co-exist, one where we look up to senior executives and see only confidence and clarity of direction, and a simultaneous reality where these same individuals feel that they are fakes about to be 'found out'. Knowing this might help you rethink your own situation. It's helpful to know the secret that many people who appear to have their careers entirely on track spend some of their time worrying whether they have any skills at all worth offering.

## REVISIT THE EVIDENCE LOCKER

Believing you are a fake is all about concealing evidence from yourself.

Senior executives worry when they attend assessment centres and take tests. They have been using numerical reasoning for decades, and yet the prospect of a test makes them feel as if they're looking over a precipice, worried that somehow their working history will mean nothing if their test results are poor.

The same thing happens with those who have been out of the workplace because of family responsibilities, health issues, or study. It's common to find people locked into the idea that they have few useful skills. They find it genuinely hard to identify achievements, not because of memory problems, but simply because their minds have overlaid a huge filter between history and perception.

Give your brain half a chance and it will choose to forget most of the times when you made a difference, averted disaster, or came up with a creative solution. It's natural. In victim mode (see Chapter 6) your brain looks, like radar, for enemy objects, not friendly data.

You have to force-feed your picture of yourself with the right material. This isn't about faking it, but drawing on treasures in your past. Try these approaches:

1. Revisit work logs, diaries, and project summaries to re-capture the contribution you made.
2. Dig out (or ask for) affidavits and recommendations, particularly from people you delighted.
3. Write out a new work history, without filtering, to build up evidence of achievement.
4. Ask friends who know you well to read it through, add to it, and (explicitly) remind you where you excel.

## Putting it all together

Some of us are remarkably thin-skinned creatures. Author Susie Boyt talked on Radio 4 in January 2014 about the intense sensitivity of childhood: 'if someone left a bit of mustard on the edge of the plate my heart really went out to it'. Imposterism, as the trait is known, is the natural extension of that sensitivity. It's a rarely disclosed vulnerability experienced by people in demanding, senior roles. Often these roles lack a natural peer group to provide feedback or constructive criticism. It is a form of self-talk that gives weight to the way we see ourselves when we are at a low ebb (see Chapter 9).

Ultimately it's about placing a barrier between yourself and reality. If you feel that you're putting on an act you'll never listen to feedback, because you'll believe that people are describing the role, not you. You won't make efforts to develop and change (what's the point if your fakery is about to be uncovered?).

Getting to grips with why you feel an imposter starts by understanding that you're far from alone. There's a lot of it out there, particularly in the same tough, resolute senior staff you've been admiring for some time. Many feel it, few reveal it — except sometimes to trusted friends.

Be different. Own up to it, to yourself and at least one person you trust, and then let it go. At the point of being hired everyone adopts a slightly glossier image than they feel, and we all sense risk doing something for the first time (see Chapter 20). However if you have held down a job for years, delivered against targets, received positive appraisals, helped colleagues, generated new ideas, and delighted the odd customer along the way — believe it all. The evidence is overwhelmingly in your favour. Phoney? Not guilty.

# 20 Fake it, but just a little

> 'Be enthusiastic. Remember the placebo effect – 30% of medicine is showbiz.' **Ronald Spark**

> 'Whenever you are asked if you can do a job, tell 'em, "Certainly I can!" Then get busy and find out how to do it.' **Theodore Roosevelt**

> 'If you don't like something, change it. If you can't change it, change your attitude.' **Maya Angelou**

> 'The thing always happens that you really believe in; and the belief in a thing makes it happen.' **Frank Lloyd Wright**

> 'Take the first step in faith. You don't have to see the whole staircase. Just take the first step.' **Martin Luther King Junior**

Television presents a very odd picture of working life. Programmes like *The Apprentice* show candidates bluffing with huge confidence but little hard evidence. Another favourite TV formula is to throw a novice into the deep end and require them to pretend basic competence in a job.

This might bring to mind the phrase 'fake it until you make it': look and sound as if you know what you're doing until reality catches up with image. In fact there's some wisdom in this, as the first technique below reveals, but there are dangers too. Firstly, if you really know you're faking it you may unconsciously be setting yourself traps, by being over-vigilant around questions that might expose the truth. You can fake confidence and impact, but not

99

knowledge or experience, so it's dangerous to claim ability levels which will be revealed as sham by your work performance.

There's a big difference between choosing to 'blag it', in current terminology, and feeling guilty because you're a fake. One is about a bravado performance, relying on a rich mix of improvisation, charm and cheekiness. Feeling that you're a fake (see Chapter 19) is about allowing your vulnerable side to entirely shape the way you see yourself.

Faking it a little means taking controlled risks in new situations. We all do it. When you walk into a room full of strangers, you have no idea how they will react to you, but you know you improve the chances of an attentive, respectful welcome if you strike the right mix of openness and credibility. You adopt a persona, you behave slightly differently to the way you behaved in the car park. You put spin on what reserves you have available. If you have your wits about you, you decide to look and act calm, measured, and approachable.

Faking it gets you into trouble and leaves you disconnected from an objective sense of what you're really capable of achieving. On the other hand, operating in the adventurous part of your comfort zone may be the only way to start something new.

## ACT THE PART WHEN PRESENTING

Prepared resilience means doing everything you can to avoid falling on your face in new circumstances. Rehearsal and planning help, but getting your mind 'in the zone' beforehand is also critical. You can't claim knowledge or experience you don't possess, but you can learn to look and sound as if you're travelling in the right direction.

When making a presentation or speech, work hardest on your initial impact. You're probably scratching your head about what you will say, but *how* you get your message across matters even more. An audience decides whether you're worth its attention in 30 seconds. Looking the part helps: smart and comfortable is what you're aiming for. Walk slowly and calmly to the place you're going to speak from. Don't straighten your clothes, shuffle papers, cough, test the microphone or any of the clichéd behaviours that shout out 'average, nervous speaker' – walk on as if you have done it a thousand times before.

Your first 30 words or so make all the difference. Plan this exactly, like all good speakers. Don't tell them your name if you've already been introduced, and don't give a rambling introduction or pitch a weak joke. Just be really clear: 'I'm here today to talk to you about…'. A punchy closing phrase also leaves an audience with a sense that you have delivered. Even if you speak from notes, learn the opening and closing phrases by heart, and look your audience in the eye when you say the words.

In other contexts, too, entering a room calmly and without fluster communicates professionalism and credibility. What's more, acting the part is a great way of believing you can do what you're there to do: controlled, positive body language directs you as much as your audience.

## SAY 'USUALLY'

When pitching for work you may be asked if you've done something like this before. It's a reasonable question: few organizations want to be guinea pigs or to run the risk of untested approaches.

If you've never done something before and state explicitly that you have, you're simply a fraud. The difficulty arises when you have done something similar. For example when people switch from salaried to self-employed work they often find themselves looking for consultancy projects. If asked 'what projects have you completed recently?' the answer could be zero, but in reality you will have handled tasks like this many times before within one or more of the jobs listed on your CV. The difference is that when you're in a full-time job you use different language to describe these work activities. Your customers may have been internal customers, your projects the routine aspects of a role. In reality you do know what you're doing – you know how to scope out a project, agree objectives, plan, execute, and review – but normally that stuff was buried inside a job title.

On these occasions many people starting out say something like 'what I usually do is …'. You've done it, but it had a different label, so don't undersell your abilities.

## BE AUTHENTIC

The real downside of 'fake it' thinking is you believe you should be somebody else. On occasions, it can help to play a role. If it helps to feel like Daniel Craig or Angelina Jolie when you walk into a client's premises, go with that. You're not doing an impression – you're borrowing a kind of energy from a screen image to boost your confidence.

Learning from other people's behaviours adds to your business toolkit. There are some pretty slick operators out there and you can improve what you do by adapting their style. 'Adapting' is the key phrase here – simple mimicry sounds false. You're borrowing; body language, style and poise, the ability to create a strong first impression. This isn't faking it, but making the best of what you have available to you.

Interview candidates are often given the meaningless advice 'be yourself' – it sounds great, but doesn't help nervous people. Better coaching shows you how to reveal *the best version of you*, and bring that alive in front of whatever audience you're trying to convince.

### Putting it all together

The big danger with faking it is that you achieve only surface confidence. You can't maintain it for long because it's paper-thin, a flimsy disguise. A couple of probing questions and you've got nothing left in your locker. Equally, 'faking it' can simply mean 'winging it' – being unprepared and unconvincing. Think carefully about the consequences in either scenario; you could be setting yourself to fail and denting your resilience.

Appropriate role play (which is what faking it is really about) allows you to see yourself in a more constructive light in order to communicate important evidence of your ability. You're not there simply to impress, but to gain commitment, win a sale, get a job offer, or influence someone's choices.

So the big issue is how risky, how much of a fake are you going to be, and who are you trying to kid? There's a big difference, for example, between telling lies about your work history and reframing your experience so someone else can see how you can help them.

If your sense of faking it rests on the idea that you really need to pretend to be somebody else, think again. Carrying that off is hard work, and although it might get you an instant 'yes', you still have to deliver further down the line. Having a reputation as fake sticks, and it's seriously bad for business. Don't feel you need to pretend to be somebody else when the best you is available, and far more authentic.

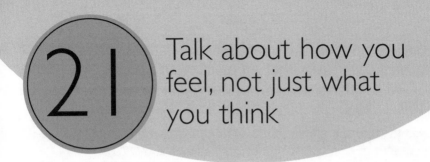

# Talk about how you feel, not just what you think

>  'A person is, among all else, a material thing, easily torn and not easily mended.' Ian McEwan

> 'Anyone who has a continuous smile on his face conceals a toughness that is almost frightening.' Greta Garbo

> 'Never apologize for showing your feelings. When you do, you are apologizing for the truth.' José N. Harris

> 'The most important things are the hardest things to say. They are the things you get ashamed of because words diminish your feelings – words shrink things that seem timeless when they are in your head to no more than living size when they are brought out.' Stephen King

> 'Half our mistakes in life arise from feeling where we ought to think, and thinking where we ought to feel.' John Churton Collins

The problems we take home from work vary. Some just require time, concentration and patience. Others are intellectual challenges which, although we complain about them, are often in fact entertaining puzzles. The biggest problems we take home are rarely just about hard work or problem solving. You might be reflecting on a difficult conversation you had today, or something stressful you have to do tomorrow; these are problems we carry with a heavy heart, because they turn us inside out emotionally.

Complex work is often emotional work. If your role is to communicate, influence, control, or manage change, you interact with emotional responses, both your own and those of others. When emotional work goes well, you get a high: people are pleased, switched on, committed, having fun. When it goes badly, people take the pieces home with them as emotional baggage.

Dealing with baggage requires good self-monitoring and a willingness to be open to one of the most important dimensions of your working life: your feelings. Discussing how you feel inevitably requires exposing a vulnerable side. The fact that a work event has triggered an uncomfortable emotional response is not something to which everyone readily admits.

Talking about feelings of vulnerability isn't a sign of weakness. It's an important stage in self-awareness and resilience. It can assist problem solving, but more than anything else it's a way of separating external from internal pressures. Identifying the problem is one task, but honestly engaging with the feelings it provokes helps you see how much you might get in the way, and what support you need to come to a sound decision.

Talking can be a way to resolve problems that go round your head in circles, recognizing that the issues that won't leave you alone often have a large emotional element. You may feel you can't move forward because of lack of information, but the main reason may be fear of uncertainty, or worrying about how others think of you. Naming your feelings is often about identifying the true underlying causes of worry.

## DEAL WITH FEELINGS AND FACTS SEPARATELY

Workplace discussions often confuse two different dimensions. People pretend or believe that they are talking about facts, but they are really finding expression for feelings (see Chapter 4). Sometimes we generalize: 'it's frustrating' rather than 'I'm frustrated'. At other times we use language which appears logical, for example 'the obvious solution is …' rather than 'the solution I am most comfortable with is …'. Another strategy is to enlist ghost supporters ('people are telling me that …') rather than saying how *you* feel about a situation.

If you're facilitating or managing a discussion on a difficult topic, try two complementary meeting strategies to help everyone be clear about feelings and facts:

1. Talk about feelings first. People often conceal feelings behind what appear to be clear-headed pros and cons, so sometimes it's healthy to get the true motivation in the spotlight. Start by asking people to put the facts aside for a minute and say, just in one sentence, how they feel about the issue.
2. Get all the negative stuff out. Good planning needs to take account of what might go wrong, but is often derailed even at the implementation stage by people who can only see snags, problems and the downside. Make a ground rule – as a group you will look exhaustively at problems, and then agree to move on to 'what if?' then 'how …' without returning ever again to the problem page.

## PRACTISE TALKING ABOUT HOW YOU FEEL

When people say they find it difficult to talk about their feelings they often mean that they haven't yet found a safe space (see below) or the right person. Sometimes they haven't found the language. In a safe environment you don't have to find the 'right' words; sounds and gestures may accurately show how you feel. The important word is 'show' – in so many areas of society we are conditioned to repress and hide feelings.

Learn to talk about your feelings more objectively and with a greater understanding of impact on others. 'I'm angry with you' or 'you make me irritated' are deeply challenging statements triggering a defensive and equally emotional response in the listener. Your anger may, after all, be entirely your problem. Sometimes it's appropriate to say 'when you say X, what I feel is Y' because there the relationship between cause and effect is open to discussion. Even safer territory is to focus on behaviour or language rather than saying something critical of the person: 'when you said "you've lost the plot" what I heard was a suggestion that I am under-prepared for team briefings … have I got that right?'.

# FIND A SAFE SPACE

A small minority never express feelings to anyone. Most people unload their feelings in a space that feels safe. This might be the patient listening of a partner or friend, or a counsellor's meeting room. It might be an inappropriate outlet – taking frustration out on a customer or anger home to your children.

A safe space involves the right place and the right people. Sounding off about your work online may be damagingly inappropriate. Your life partner may not be the right person: talking about work frustrations may make your partner feel that your job is insecure or you're about to leave it.

A safe space enables conversation where you can speak freely without damaging relationships, diminishing yourself, or denting your reputation. In general therefore a frank discussion with your boss expressing strong feelings is rarely a good idea. You might be able to have that kind of conversation with a mentor who works in your organization, but in some cases you'll need to find people who are not work colleagues.

Pick positive-minded people who are good listeners. They need to understand their role: simply to listen while you download. Their job is not to top your story with one of their own or generalize about how difficult life is for everyone. Pick people who listen first and offer solutions tentatively. Remember this isn't primarily about solving problems – it's about exploring your feelings properly so you don't get in the way of your own solutions.

## Putting it all together

You know people who constantly reveal their emotional state. Often this is a surface level running commentary ('I'm fed up') rather than real disclosure ('I've just had a conversation that made me feel stupid and humiliated').

Others keep information about their emotional life under wraps. The danger here is that you can come across as a cold automaton who is not really engaged, or seen as calculating and manipulative. It's even more common that work colleagues assume you're happy enough simply because you don't say otherwise.

You are not your feelings. Expressing anger doesn't make you an angry person any more than being hungry makes you a glutton. Sometimes it's helpful to describe feelings as a passing state: 'right now I'm feeling isolated and let down' locks you in far less than 'my colleagues hate me'.

We can all get better at talking about how we feel. You might think that talking about yourself should be easy. Just being listened to can help you feel supported, and it is a good cure for a sense of isolation. It works both ways; if you open up, it encourages others to see you as someone they can confide in.

Expressing sadness, elation, fear, apprehension are important parts of our stories. Talk about your feelings, but don't let it become a litany. Talking about how you feel too often, repeatedly, without engaging in a conversation about what happens next, is simply about wanting to put yourself at the centre of things.

# 22 Modify your behaviours under pressure

> 'Anger is an acid that can do more harm to the vessel in which it is stored than to anything on which it is poured.'
> Mark Twain

> 'Experience – the wisdom that enables us to recognize in an undesirable old acquaintance the folly that we have already embraced.' Ambrose Bierce

> 'Resentment is like drinking poison and waiting for the other person to die.' Carrie Fisher

> 'Most of the successful people I've known are the ones who do more listening than talking.' Bernard M. Baruch

> 'An apology is the superglue of life. It can repair just about anything.' Lynn Johnston

Time and experience have given you glimpses into your own personality. You may also have some insights into your natural preferences from direct feedback, or from psychometric testing. Whether these glimpses reveal truths depends on your level of self-awareness, especially the realization that others may have a very different take on life.

Such information can provide powerful insights into your own strengths and limitations. Understanding how you see the world may give you insights into why you find it easier to get on with some work colleagues rather than others, and may help to explain fundamental differences in working style. As Chapter 27 reveals, there will almost certainly be parts of your psychological make-up that you can't see, but colleagues can.

Psychometric test users are often interested in the way we are likely to revert to type under pressure – in other words, how your underlying nature is more likely to reveal itself when you are emotionally challenged. Personality traits (for example, irritability or a mild obsession with accuracy) can be masked in normal working conditions (you may be happy to overlook errors in early drafts of shared text knowing that you will give the document a final proofread). If however you introduce additional pressures (equipment failure, conflicting deadlines, a hangover) then it's more likely that underlying characteristics will reveal themselves.

A good example would be to think about the way quiet, reflective people operate. In normal practice they may enjoy and even prefer their own company much of the time, but in a typical work situation they can happily rub alongside other types of people they wouldn't normally include in their social circle. However give this kind of person something demanding and complicated, and you will see them seek quiet and solitude to think things through.

More extrovert types, on the other hand, may well suppress their dominant side. They will take the time to delegate and consult carefully when pressure is light, but turn up the heat and they may start to be uncompromising and directive, particularly if they believe they have the best solution in mind.

## GET OUT OF THE BOX

Current thinking on personality suggests that we can all to some extent shift out of the 'types' or boxes that some tests threaten to push us into. Human beings are more complex and varied than any test summary, and also more flexible. If you have the right mindset, listen to feedback, and think about the needs and reactions of others, you can adjust your behaviours. In one sense this describes a great deal of our learning – we don't simply repeat actions and behaviours, but adapt them in the light of feedback from our environment.

Work from the assumption that your behaviours are more flexible than your preferences. You know it's true. It's possible to be charming, diplomatic, to engage in small talk, even if you hate doing so. If the motivation is right, you can demonstrate behaviours outside your normal range.

Not everyone can do this, and none of us has complete flexibility. Unless you are a rare chameleon, you can only go some way outside your range. For example, if you're a rules-led, process-oriented person who likes to do things by the book, it's hard to adopt a relaxed attitude to detail. What we can do, however, is to appoint surrogates to act in our place. If you have a document that has to be 100% accurate and you're not the best proofreader, find someone who is. If you need something to be said diplomatically, either rehearse the words (see Chapter 24) or identify someone who has the skills and people 'radar' you don't possess (see Chapter 40).

# REJECT NEGATIVE SCRIPTS

In their book *The Power Of Resilience* (McGraw-Hill, 2004) Robert Brooks and Sam Goldstein write about resilient mindsets and negative scripts. Following a negative script means adopting the same counterproductive actions and behaviours time after time (for example, 'I'm not going to blow my own trumpet – if the boss can't tell if I'm doing a good job she should find out for herself!').

Negative scripts can easily keep running like a perpetual autocue, even when you have the power to change things for the better. Brooks and Goldstein suggest that a major step towards resilience is to recognize that we are the authors of our lives, able to change these scripts. They argue that 'resilient individuals are those who have a set of assumptions or attitudes about themselves that influence their behaviours and the skills they develop and that negative scripts get in the way of this process.

Look at your own negative scripts. They often emerge as your 'rules' about how things should be done ('if you want something doing properly, do it yourself') or how the world operates ('it's not about what you know but who you know'). They emerge in the daily one-liners we use in work about bosses, bureaucracy and customers, often wittily cynical ('school would be fine if it wasn't for the pupils ... and the staff'). The problem is that repeated negative statements are a way of repeatedly telling yourself that nothing can change.

# FIND CALM LANGUAGE

One of the reasons we avoid conflict is that we feel that the only way we can express what we feel or think is in conflict language (see Chapter 23).

Where things are not working for you, you need to find the right language to deal with them. If the only way you can talk about problems is by complaining, you will only achieve the things you can gain from a complaints process. Similarly, if the only way you can move forward is to criticize a colleague, you will get results limited to that process.

Calm language requires you to listen. Listening isn't just about receiving, it shapes the way you respond. Listen to the self-talk that gets in the way, and listen most of all to those flash-summaries that tip you towards blame or panic. Listen to words before you speak them, and find calm language.

Calm language is not just spoken calmly, but also finds neutral terminology. So if someone talks about catastrophe, look at what's still working (see Chapter 3). If you hear anything labelled a mistake, or blame is attached, start by looking at what has happened.

## Putting it all together

Don't accept the idea that you are hemmed in by your personality. The cliché 'you can't teach an old dog new tricks' is disproved every day. As Chapter 7 shows, even the most damaged individuals can experience a turnaround in their mindset and confidence. Human beings have evolved to be adaptive so they can thrive in a huge range of climatic, cultural, political and economic environments. We're good at flexing behaviours and attitudes to make things work.

So saying 'this is how I am, take it or leave it' goes completely against the grain. It is really saying 'I refuse to listen to my own instincts' – a denial of your fundamental abilities to observe and change. In a world where radical change is the dominant characteristic in technology and systems, this is heard as the statement 'I've stopped listening'. Exhaustion may make this an understandable response, but this mindset quickly makes individuals look stuck in their ways and highly dispensable.

Learn new behaviours. Try them out like a new outfit. Some will fit, some won't. Don't experiment in critical situations, but in low-key contexts where getting it wrong has limited consequences.

As you adapt, watch out for self-talk that tells you something is impossible, and beware negative scripts.

If you do one thing, work towards calm language. It's a great behaviour modifier, because it requires you to slow down a reaction process, take stock, and distinguish fact from feelings (see Chapter 4).

# 23 Engage with conflict where you need to

&#x275C;&#x275C; *'Conflict is inevitable, but combat is optional.'* Max Lucado

&#x275C;&#x275C; *'Conflict is the gadfly of thought. It stirs us to observation and memory. It instigates to invention. It shocks us out of sheep like passivity, and sets us at noting and contriving.'* John Dewey

&#x275C;&#x275C; *'Don't ever take a fence down until you know why it was put up.'* Robert Frost

&#x275C;&#x275C; *'Never cut what you can untie.'* Joseph Joubert

&#x275C;&#x275C; *'Courage is what it takes to stand up and speak. Courage is also what it takes to sit down and listen.'* Winston Churchill

You may fear conflict because you don't like to trigger assertiveness in other people. You're more afraid of their immediate response than the long-term consequences; short-term gain (no one shouts at you) leads to long-term pain (being in an uncomfortable situation). You feel diminished – you've allowed yourself to be beaten into the ground, possibly giving others the impression you're weak.

We vary in how much we dread conflict. Some people relish heated debate, others never say anything in their own defence, never question a decision, never send something back in a restaurant. You may firmly believe that good relationships should not involve arguments.

Sometimes we think we're avoiding conflict but in reality we're concealing it in manipulative behaviours – for example giving others the silent treatment (in the hope of making them feel guilty). This passive-aggressive behaviour merely postpones resolution, sometimes indefinitely.

We develop countless strategies to avoid conflict. The result isn't always negative; sometimes getting on with people is what matters, and good relationships mean ignoring small points of tension. However, there are also situations when conflict avoidance means being repeatedly submissive. For example, where someone shouts at you to get your attention, or where your boss blames you for his mistakes and takes credit for your best ideas. In this kind of situation you need to ask who gains, and who loses – where is the power here?

As Chapter 21 shows, it's important to be honest with yourself about how you feel, especially in situations which you feel can only be resolved through conflict. This is rarely the case. Other tools are available: patience, charm, humour, and cool, clear explanations about how you feel.

## DON'T BE A DOORMAT

You may choose to avoid conflict in order to maintain good working relationships. This may be a sound strategy if it maintains healthy relationships. The important question is whether it's appropriate to concede. What happens if your perspective is never taken seriously? The danger is that by using only one strategy to maintain the relationship, you devalue it. Agree sometimes, but at other times express a different view. Even the most contradictory statements can be pitched diplomatically.

Constantly being the one who gives in makes you a doormat. Others sense they can make ever more unreasonable demands. As you feel increasingly like a compliant victim, you allow your picture of your own worth to be eroded, day by day. The mat just inside your front door doesn't just say 'welcome', it says 'treat me as roughly as you like'.

You might think that being a doormat is a purely private state of affairs. It isn't; workplace sharks sense it like blood in the water. You'll find that you are given increasingly mundane, possibly even humiliating, tasks to do, and you'll quickly be written off as a serious player. Although you feel you're playing by office rules, what you're actually doing is accepting someone else's picture of work as a dog pack, and in doing so missing out on opportunities to grow and succeed.

## THINK REACTIONS AND CONSEQUENCES

Conflict avoidance is triggered by the dark movie you run in your head when you face the need to oppose someone's thinking. Inevitably, you think about consequences with your gut as much as your brain, but this means that you see one-dimensional outcomes. Therefore you can sometimes achieve breakthroughs when a friend asks 'what's the worst thing that can happen?'.

How you work is as important as what you get out of it. All work is a deal – a deal you re-negotiate from time to time. However, you need to think about how people will react when you push back, no matter how gently. When you think about consequences, watch you imagine only negative outcomes. You'll say 'I don't want to go complaining to my boss ...' or 'I don't want to stir up trouble...'.

If you need to say something about unresolved conflict, consider carefully who to approach. Think about the kind of person you have to tell. Is he or she also a conflict avoider? When is the best timing? Consider also the likely reactions of your boss. Are you in fact supposed to be responsible for sorting these kinds of problems out for yourself? If not, what do you expect a busy manager to do? Most managers dislike receiving this kind of information because they often find it very difficult to implement a solution. You may, however, get a different reaction if you say 'I don't expect you do to anything about this, but it's important to me to tell you that ...'.

Think about consequences, too. What is likely to happen next? If you complain about a co-worker who then behaves worse as a consequence, what will you do about it?

## DON'T CONFUSE CONFLICT WITH ABUSE

Sometimes when people talk about 'conflict' they really mean workplace abuse. They may experience bullying or harassment, and don't know what to do about it. In other circumstances they may feel a moral obligation to be a whistle-blower, but again they are too frightened to take action.

Few people have the prepared strength to deal with high levels of intimidation in the workplace, so the fact that you didn't know how to respond at the time is perfectly understandable. What matters is that you take the right steps afterwards. This is about boundaries; either you set them (by challenging the behaviours) or someone else does. Silently tolerating aggressive or inappropriate behaviour merely encourages perpetrators to believe they are operating in a bubble where no one can really see or hear them. Take advice, informally at first, but take steps to protect yourself.

## Putting it all together

Constant conflict is tiring and counterproductive, but conflict avoidance is often really about an unhealthy acceptance that the loudest voice in the room makes most sense. Conflict is not always problematic. Often conflict and creativity are partners: sharp debate can lead to smart ideas.

Conflict is real when it spills out of context. For example barristers in court seem locked in intense rivalry, but will josh each other affectionately in the corridor. Creative types appear willing to fight to the death over a brand name, and will later be convivial in the pub. Colleagues can trade insults that sound deeply wounding to an outsider. Where conflict leaks out of context is where you go home cursing your colleagues and complaining about work every evening.

Being honest about conflict often means being honest with yourself about why you avoid it: you feel are going to lose. If you're paralysed by worrying about the fallout from conflict, you're already losing. If conflict is present, it's present – avoiding it is attempting to pretend that another universe co-exists. If you choose to be compliant or to keep your views to yourself, make it a conscious decision, and review it every time. Repeated, habitual conflict avoidance merely puts you into submissive mode.

# 24 Manage difficult relationships better

>  *'Most people do not listen with the intent to understand; they listen with the intent to reply.'* Stephen R. Covey

> *'Listening looks easy, but it's not simple. Every head is a world.'* Cuban Proverb

> *'If you understood everything I said, you'd be me.'* Miles Davis

> *'Learning would be exceedingly laborious, not to mention hazardous, if people had to rely solely on the effects of their own actions to inform them what to do. Fortunately, most human behaviour is learned observationally through modelling: from observing others one forms an idea of how new behaviours are performed, and on later occasions this coded information serves as a guide for action.'* Albert Bandura

> *'I don't know the key to success, but the key to failure is trying to please everybody.'* Bill Cosby

Remember the joking response to the question 'how are you?' – *I'm fine, it's everyone else I worry about.* We have all worked with people who have convinced themselves that they are the only sane and competent person in their workplace. Even just a hint of that is a great way of deflecting anything that sounds like criticism.

Chapter 38 shows you how to attract support actively, and many other chapters reveal the way that positive relationships inject resilience, and damaged relationships or the absence of supportive interaction takes it away.

Difficult relationships are often at the heart of many forms of work unhappiness. Indeed, people will often put up with very dull jobs if they enjoy the company of the people around them and feel respect for the way they are managed. Others will only put up with overbearing management styles or the sniping of colleagues for the sake of a job they find intrinsically interesting and rewarding.

We need to be clear what we mean by *difficult*. Some conversations are difficult because they are hard to hear – for example where someone is discussing your underperformance, or where you have to ask someone to modify their behaviours. Others are difficult because there is 'history': you may simply be asking for a month-end report, but that request causes irritation. You may have got to the stage where anything you say or hear sounds like a criticism or a threat.

It's unwise to ignore failing relationships; repeated misunderstandings and over-interpretation don't just wreck office harmony, they get in the way of results, damage careers, and can easily put you on the back foot so that you miss other things which are even more important. If your team needs make a big effort to save the day, you don't have time to try to patch up differences or deal with simmering discontent, and any motivating speeches about teamwork will sound like an empty clichés.

Deal with relationship problems early, taking advice if you need it, and thinking ahead all the time about the conversations required.

## SPOT THE RELATIONSHIP DEAL-BREAKERS

What gets in the way of success for you? This important coaching question can flag up many simple factors which get in the way of doing a good job. It's rare that the answer doesn't say something about people. Typical people factors getting in the way of success in today's workplace include:

- Back-biting, sniping, and silo mentality (see Chapter 8 on organizational politics).
- Inadequate or late communication.
- Poor working relationships in a team.
- Being micro-managed by an over-anxious boss.
- Having managers who do not set clear and consistent goals.

The critical issue is how far weak relationships impact on your work performance. Think back to a time when the context was different: how did that allow you to work differently?

Every workplace has some people problems; good judgement requires you to address the ones that seriously get in the way of results. Identify the relationship issues that get in the way of achievement. Think now about what you can do about them, perhaps through others, perhaps by biting the bullet and having a difficult conversation (see below).

## REHEARSE DIFFICULT CONVERSATIONS

If you find yourself in a difficult conversation at work without warning, try to take some time to go away and think what you want to say. Avoid the temptation to 'wing it' on the day. Doing so means you weaken your ability to sense what's going on in the room, including tone, body language, choice of words, and emotional impact.

Rehearse conversations properly, thinking about the exact words you will use – not something vague like 'I'll talk to Jill about her performance' or 'I've got to tell Mike that he's going to be made redundant'. Proper rehearsal means focusing on the actual sentences you will speak, including the words you use to set up the meeting, and the words you use right at the beginning of the conversation. Some generalized openings simply trigger a defensive response, so 'we have a problem with your commitment' puts you both into conflict mode, whereas 'how do you feel the last year has gone?' checks out territory more carefully. Avoiding vague, un-provable generalizations ('people are telling me', or 'I'm picking up').

Managers who handle these conversations well play conversations out in their imaginations in great detail, rehearsing their words, anticipating colleague reactions, and thinking about likely outcomes.

# TELL PEOPLE WHAT YOU NEED

If you're given a challenge which pushes you outside your comfort zone, find a time to talk about what you need to get from A to B. This isn't about being unrealistic about resources – most people would like more help and more time – or appearing needy. This is about thinking about how you will meet the objectives you have been set. Failing to consider the tools you need to complete the job is about setting yourself up for a fall.

Firstly, be clear about the task. If it's complicated and will take you more than a few hours to achieve, it's reasonable to scope the task out properly. Some of this will be in your own time, but it generally impresses to be able to summarize the key outcomes back to the person who is delegating the job in your direction. Negotiating time for the task, and agreeing what other work can be dropped for the moment, is also something you can do at when you accept the task.

Next, look at what you need to get the job done. This could be about direct resources such as equipment and people, but often the support you will need will be in terms of learning (how will you acquire or develop relevant skills and knowledge?). You may also need support in terms of supervision. Learn to do this with a light touch: 'I hope it's all right for me to check in with a progress report early next week?' With people you know and trust you can be even more explicit about your need for encouragement ('you know what I'm like – do tell me if I'm doing OK / making a mess of things / give me a gold star and a tick if you like what you see').

## Putting it all together

Resilience isn't achieved in isolation. It depends very heavily on relationships. Good working relationships allow you to talk about what you need, and enable you to gather support for tougher times. Resilient people tend to have at least a few core relationships of trust and support, and not too many relationships which are destructive.

A simple health check on the way work impacts on your well-being will quickly require attention to relationships. How much do you require trust and understanding – and how often do you offer the same? Is work a place where you need to develop strong relationships, even friendships, to be effective?

Whether we avoid difficult relationships or learn to manage them depends on the context. Sometimes leaving difficult people behind you is a smart move, but there comes a time when you need to find the courage and skill to have conversations that you'd rather avoid. Spotting the problems which are deal-breakers reveals the difference between background irritation and significant blocks to progress.

The other side of well-managed relationships is of course self-awareness and honesty. Soldiering on naively, unaware of your impact on others and blaming colleagues if they see things differently, quickly puts you in the 'awkward squad', which can easily lead to you being considered off message and dispensable.

Careful preparation, even thorough rehearsal, is vital for difficult conversations. Improvisation is sometimes a great communication tool, but often dangerous if you're trying to say something which someone else finds to hear.

# 25 Learn to ask for help

66 'When we give cheerfully and accept gratefully, everyone is blessed.' Maya Angelou

66 'There can be no vulnerability without risk; there can be no community without vulnerability; there can be no peace, and ultimately no life, without community.' M. Scott Peck

66 'It's not the load that breaks you down; it's the way you carry it.' Lena Horne

66 'In everyone's life, at some time, our inner fire goes out. It is then burst into flame by an encounter with another human being. We should all be thankful for those people who rekindle the inner spirit.' Albert Schweitzer

66 'Don't keep your heart safe ... be vulnerable.' John Mayer

Friends value your flaws as well as your achievements, your vulnerabilities as much as your strengths. So why do we hide them at work? The answer is that we have learned to value toughness. We work in a culture where goals have to be met and hard decisions implemented – a world where weakness gets in the way. This individualistic culture allows us freedom of choice, but the downside is a strong feeling that you're on your own.

Work today regularly requires us to multi-task and operate outside our skills range, but some of us are not very good at asking for help. There are of course those individuals who ask for help too often, signalling that they're not too good at doing things unsupervised. Others, particularly men, instinctively feel that asking for help is like a pet rolling over to reveal its soft underbelly: vulnerable to attack. We fear rejection or looking stupid. We don't want to be a burden or add to someone's workload. Ultimately we believe the corporate myth that asking for help makes you lose control and look weak.

Vulnerability is a difficult trait to handle in the modern workplace. If you're too thin-skinned you find it difficult to weather everyday change and robust feedback. If you have no vulnerability you probably find it difficult to imagine how other people feel, or what they think of you. Leaders who recognize their own vulnerability and reveal a little of it to others are often the most respected.

Look for positive role models – people higher up the food chain who have a naturally comfortable way of asking for advice or practical help. Often this is done with humour. Generally it's done with complete honesty, and not too much self-criticism. Professionals who learn this skill often have great networks of supporters.

Asking for help has many advantages. Saying that you don't fully understand something can be a helpful relationship builder. Admitting that you have bad days or sometimes feel unsure of your abilities communicates that you're human, not a corporate robot.

## ASK FOR HELP, NOT A RESCUE PACKAGE

The words you use to ask for help don't just affect outcomes, they determine how you will be remembered.

Asking for help reveals a level of vulnerability, but that doesn't need to be extreme. The problem is that putting yourself down can easily be something you habitually adopt like a verbal reflex. If you start by saying 'I've got a big problem', 'I'm out of my depth', or (like some co-workers) you flutter eyelashes in mock submissiveness, you're broadcasting helplessness.

When you seek help, remember that opening words matter. Flattery is fine, as long as you're not asking to be rescued. So 'could I pick your brain?' or 'can I run an idea by you?' are better openers – your colleague is thinking less about your vulnerability and more about the puzzle to be solved.

Drop the habit of justifying your request with small side remarks like 'I'm rubbish at spreadsheets'. You don't need to run yourself down in order to tap into someone else's expertise. Talk about what you have already tried to reinforce the idea that you are independent enough to have a go at something, but sensible enough to seek help before you go too far down the wrong path.

## OFFER MATCHED FUNDING

Let's say you're seeking new contacts to help you build business. Your little black book is largely empty, but you know some great networkers. If you go cap in hand saying 'I could do with some names' you'll receive some help, but you'll get better results talking about the problems you're trying to solve. For example, start by saying 'I'm trying to find out more about SAP' or 'I'm trying to find a great communications agency'. Adding 'I know you're the person to talk to' helps to oil the wheels.

However this approach can still sound as if you're really saying 'I can't be bothered to find out for myself'. So throw in some of the names and organizations you have already approached or discovered. If you're asking for contacts, show that you have been proactive and made some approaches yourself: 'I've already got a good list of contacts, but I wonder if you can add to them'.

## TEN TIPS FOR ASKING FOR HELP

1. Be clear why you're asking for help. Are you looking for information or knowledge? Are you trying to find out how to do something? If you're really seeking encouragement or feedback, say so honestly.
2. Don't hang about. If you're going to ask for help, ask early. If you're delegated a task, review what it will involve and think about obstacles and problems. Take time to review how you'll get round them, and consult early if you can't.

3. Don't apologize. Asking for help is about appropriate vulnerability, not helplessness.
4. Think intelligently about who you ask. The worst people are closed down, difficult to approach, and people who are likely to read a request for help as pure weakness. The best are those who actively enjoy watching others grow. (See Chapter 17 on judging who to ask.)
5. Talk about major vulnerabilities privately. We all have areas of uncertainty, sometimes real self-doubt. Learning resilience is often about talking them through, but choose a coach or a trusted mentor rather than people who may misconstrue this information or use it against you.
6. Be clear about the help you need. Saying 'I need you to talk me through the process' is clearer and less damaging than 'I don't know where to begin'.
7. Cultivate supporters. Recruit people inside and outside your workplace who can guide, challenge and encourage (see Chapter 38).
8. Thank people properly. Again, don't be tempted by melodrama ('you saved my life!'), but be explicit about how you were helped and what you achieved as a result.
9. Seek opportunities to reciprocate. Don't feel indebted or believe that you have to reciprocate immediately, but sooner or later a chance will come along to return the favour. Ignore it and you break trust.
10. Broadcast as well as receive. Becoming known as someone who can offer sound advice, short cuts, and useful information, is a great career enhancer.

**Putting it all together**

Swap the word 'vulnerable' for the word 'open' and you can see how letting your guard down from time to time is good practice. Deciding you have no weak spots is pretty close to believing you can't learn anything new. An honest vulnerability helps to build relationships of trust, and allows you to keep learning, but this doesn't mean allowing people to walk all over you (see Chapter 23 on being a doormat).

Revealing too much vulnerability acts against resilience. If you communicate fragility and a lack of ability to help yourself, interesting tasks won't be delegated in your direction, and because you need to be treated with kid gloves managers will find it easier to go elsewhere.

Being frightened to reveal vulnerability is understandable, but as you become more relaxed at work it helps to build relationships to honestly disclose the things that worry you. Make sure they are not deal-breakers though, and make sure you're not telling the wrong person. Admitting 'this is all new to me' to someone senior that you don't know very well could mean that you are taken off a project. Seeking help with the things that don't come easily is good team practice as long as you return the favour.

Pretending you have no vulnerable side makes you seem as if you have no self-awareness, and if it looks like you believe in your own perfection you may be set up to fail. The workplace has enough bear traps without setting them for yourself.

# 26 Get honest feedback

> **"** 'Feedback is the breakfast of champions.' Ken Blanchard

> **"** 'Through others we become ourselves.' Lev S. Vygotsky

> **"** 'Timidity makes a person modest. It makes him or her say, "I'm not worthy of being written up in the record of deeds in heaven or on earth." Timidity keeps people from their good. They are afraid to say, 'Yes, I deserve it.' Maya Angelou

> **"** 'Nobody can make you feel inferior without your consent.' Eleanor Roosevelt

> **"** 'Blessed are the cracked, for they shall let in the light.' Groucho Marx

A great deal of this book is about monitoring your feelings and responses. Self-checking is an important process, particularly when it comes to looking at ways your resilience is built or dampened.

The danger with self-checking is that it can be very one-dimensional: your attention is all on the way you see things. To be an effective work colleague, consultant, or family member, it helps to know your impact on others. How well we see ourselves as we are seen by others (see Chapter 27) varies considerably.

Where people don't notice their effect on the outside world it's as if they are living in a glass bubble – it lets in light, but restricts sound. Look around you in the workplace and you will see people who operate that way: impervious to external signals unless they are loud enough to crack the glass. They don't pick up 'atmosphere', and only respond when someone takes them to task or issues a formal warning.

Which is best in terms of resilience: enhanced self-awareness or an impervious, closed-down approach? There isn't a 'best', of course. The danger of being highly tuned to yourself and the way other people see you is that you hear too much self-talk. Worrying about what other people are feeling and saying about you makes you jump at shadows. On the other hand, those who have no idea of their reputation or impact are often most shocked when their job comes to an end, and most lacking in support.

Feedback isn't always straightforward. Sometimes it comes with an agenda. You may be receiving advice or criticism from someone who is very unlike you. When a colleague says 'what you should do is …', ask yourself if they are in reality advising themselves, or expecting you to become a kind of clone.

On the other hand, when you get feedback from more than one source which comes as a surprise, take it seriously. If you thought the client presentation went well but your colleague and the client take a very different view, it's probably time to stop believing your own PR and take a fresh look at how you operate.

## PICK OBJECTIVE OBSERVERS, NOT JUST FANS

It does no harm to get regular encouragement – most people could do with a lot more than they get. Positive strokes don't just make you feel good, but reinforce strengths and enhance future performance. Receiving feedback from people who like the way you do things is a healthy way of building resilience. Going into difficult situations feeling that you have a fan club behind you is no bad thing. Indeed, it's a good idea to remember positive feedback on past performance before you throw yourself into something challenging.

The downside of only listening to your support team is the danger faced by many people in public life who have risen so far up the ladder that they no longer have a peer group or wide counsellors. Unconsciously they have decided to blank out anything which is off-message. The danger (played out every week in the media) is that senior corporate and political figures who have lost touch with the way they are seen. They surround themselves with people who say that everything is golden and don't notice the rust.

We all do that when we decide to listen only to feedback we want to hear. Listening to things which make you squirm a little is highly instructive.

## ASK HOW, NOT WHAT

Imagine you've chaired a meeting today and you ask a trusted colleague for feedback on how things went. That feedback will probably be a quick summary: 'brilliant', 'OK', 'You handled that well'. It's the kind of remark we put on Twitter at the end of a meeting or working day. Pithy, but bland and short on facts.

What's fine for Twitter doesn't work quite so well for direct feedback. Ask patiently for details and facts you can work with. Therefore after saying 'how did that go?' you might take the conversation in a different direction: 'I'm not after flattery, but could you tell me what, exactly went well?' Good follow-up questions would include 'what did I do to make it work?' and 'what did I do which made the meeting go less well?'. The strongest questions are 'what should I repeat next time?' and 'what can I work on to do things better?'.

## DON'T CHANGE THE WHOLE SHOW

Next time a friend tells you about a public presentation they gave which took a nose dive, ask them (when they're feeling strong enough) what went wrong. Normally they start with what, not how (see above) – they say 'it was a disaster' or 'I was rubbish'. With their permission, ask them to run the event by you in slow motion: 'what was the first thing you said?' … 'how did you feel just after you started speaking?'.

In many cases you will find that the speaker dropped the plan for the talk within two minutes of beginning. They had a script, well-prepared, but they decided to go off in a different direction.

Confident speakers can of course improvise, even abandon all plans, and still have an audience eating out of their hand. Average speakers, however, tend to be influenced by their first impression of audience response, which is usually entirely inaccurate. Next they start to make adjustments – usually with dramatic consequences. They over-run, finish far too soon, cut out their best material, and otherwise look and sound like someone who can't wait to get offstage.

When the performance (or interview, or conversation) goes off balance, the temptation is to alter your balance completely. It's rather like standing in a rowing boat; the boat tips one way, you put all your weight in the other direction, and you're over the side.

Over-compensation means that you try to change everything, immediately. Sometimes this is because you're given bland, universal feedback ('you need to sharpen up your act'), but at other times you may be given (or assume) a long list of faults and try to change them all. If you do that you will have no idea what is getting you improved results. Focus on one or two important changes, try them out, then get further feedback before trying further adjustments.

## Putting it all together

Watch people develop in their careers. Simply because they have to rub up alongside others, the membrane of their personal bubble thins out, and they increasingly hear information from the outside world. This ability to seek out (and really listen to) feedback is a sign of maturity as well as growth – it means you no longer trust your internal myth-making. This could be either that you can do nothing wrong, or nothing right; myths generally come in black and white.

Honest feedback is negative and positive – it's good to see your blind spots, but some are poor at accepting praise. The important thing is that we encourage feedback. Feedback is vital in any process of learning, but self-monitoring is rarely efficient: you may think you are speeding ahead, but you may have missed some vital stages in the process. Equally, you may feel that nothing is working and you need someone to remind you of your successes.

Feedback isn't always accurate – even the most robust 360-degree surveys can sometimes allow hidden agendas to play out. Find a small range of people you trust enough to give a straight answer to the question 'how do others see me?'. You don't have to like the answer to act upon it.

Ask for detail in feedback that you can act upon, and start by focusing on changing one or two behaviours which matter. Often this means listening more and talking less. Don't distract yourself with worry if you get mixed feedback – if the overall picture says you're doing well enough, that's fine for now.

# See yourself as others see you – and shape your reputation

❝ *'Everything that irritates us about others can lead us to an understanding of ourselves.'* Carl Jung

❝ *'When you're different, sometimes you don't see the millions of people who accept you for what you are. All you notice is the person who doesn't.'* Jodi Picoult

❝ *'At ev'ry word a reputation dies.'* Alexander Pope, 'The Rape of the Lock'

❝ *'Unhappiness is best defined as the difference between our talents and our expectations.'* Edward de Bono

❝ *'The more credit you give away, the more will come back to you. The more you help others, the more they will want to help you.'* Brian Tracy

Jane is your CEO. This morning she is standing by the coffee machine with a group of colleagues, and your name comes up in conversation. What is said? The things that are said in the next few minutes could dictate your future. Busy decision-makers often make one-off decisions based on short recommendations, or equally brief expressions of doubt.

How would your co-workers describe your working style? Would they describe the things you're good at, the things you've done well? Will they talk about how you are now, what you used to be, or what you could achieve if you pulled your finger out?

Personal reputations are built on sound bites. Too many individuals try to navigate their careers without knowing how they are seen by other people who can make a difference to their futures. This group may be wider than you think – not just senior staff in your own organization but key people in your industry, and important intermediaries such as executive recruiters. One of the ways you know that the hidden job market is working in your favour, for example, is that your name comes up in conversation when you are not present.

You may worry too much or too little about how you are perceived; either will mislead you unless you get good feedback. Here a mentor arguably has greater value than a coach. Find someone relatively senior, actively interested in your development, and – most importantly – better than you at decoding the organization.

You may have done an exceptional job this year. Who is aware of that fact? People believe that if they work hard, progression will follow automatically. When it doesn't, it's easy to sound jaded or cynical, and this picture leaks through to decision-makers. Alternatively, you may have a high or low picture of your impact and performance. Taking steps to check how far that matches the reality shared by co-workers is a vital step in self-awareness. Addressing key problems heads off trouble, and understanding why you are valued by your employer helps bank confidence.

## OPEN THE JOHARI WINDOW

The Johari Window concept was created in the 1950s by Joseph Luft and Harrington Ingham. The idea is that we are conscious of part of our lives, and unconscious of other parts. The Window is often expressed as a four-box grid:

| 1. Known to self and to others(open) | 2. Not known to self but known to others(blind) |
|---|---|
| 3. Known to self and not to others(closed) | 4. Not known to self or others (dark) |

This model offers much to reflect on, but for now look just at boxes 1 and 2. Firstly, what do people see in you that you don't yet see in yourself? To accept information in this zone requires maturity and a little courage; you'll hear about strengths, but you will also hear about traits you weren't aware of. Sometimes these are allowable weaknesses (e.g. you're untidy, but you're very creative), but at times your working style may be damaging relationships or, worse, preventing other people doing their jobs properly.

Although feedback in this area can come as a shock, it's good to know how people label you. This can range from inaccurate cliché to a spot-on summary. You can be aware of these opinions without accepting them. If someone says 'I see you as a good organizer' that may be in comparison only with themselves. However if someone says 'I get feedback that you motivate people in your team' or 'I have noticed that you rarely speak in meetings', that's probably solid evidence.

Discovering the *you* that others see can be painful, so find supportive colleagues who can tell you straight without leaving you feeling demolished. Consider how far you actively contribute to what people say about you. You may think this is outside your control, but this chapter reveals you may have far more influence than you think.

## DON'T WAIT FOR YOUR NEXT APPRAISAL

Your image isn't shaped by things you do all the year round at work, but by brief moments of visibility. For example when giving a presentation when your MD is in the room, or you make a big impact in a new team, or tracking down vital research or great new resources.

Dump any lingering misconceptions about how people make progress in organizations. We'd like to believe that people get promoted because of annual appraisals or hard work, but these usually just confirm that you're competent. Many are perplexed at the 'something extra' they need to put in to be noticed. You work hard and stack up achievements, but the big question is, who notices? You could follow the crowd by working hard and keeping your head down, but will this get you promoted? And if things falter, how long before start to sound jaded and cynical, and this becomes your water-cooler reputation?

# DECIDE ON THE MESSAGES YOU WANT TO TRAVEL

How much is said when your name is mentioned? When someone criticizes a colleague this can last for what seems like hours, but listen to how much is said when someone is recommended. Most people seem to pass on just three or four pieces of information – they don't want to sound as if they are over-selling.

A small amount of this might be about how easy you are to get on with, but in general those three or four phrases cover the main reasons someone might want to recommend you – your high-level skills, your expertise, industry or technical knowledge, or your contacts. You may have 200 pieces of information in your CV, but in a water-cooler conversation only three or four of them will come up.

What others hear about you is far from random. It's all down to you. Focus on what you want people to remember about you, and what messages you want to them to pass on. If you tell all your contacts you're bored with your job and hate your boss, that becomes your market reputation. So choose which three or four key messages you want to get across (probably close to the main straplines on your LinkedIn page), tell people consistently, and this will be what travels.

## Putting it all together

Resilience relies heavily on confidence, and one of the ways you can push someone's confidence down from 100% to zero is to give them a harsh wake-up call about the way they are seen by others. A positive version of this, when you discover how much you are valued, is of course a great boost. A key step is to understand which of your qualities and behaviours others talk about, and how they condense your contribution into short sound bites.

The resilient self leaves less of this business of lifting up and flattening to chance by taking feedback. You may be intuitive enough to sense how others see you, but be careful – you could be making a lot of assumptions. Extroverts tend to assume that others like the noisy, boisterous behaviours they bring to the workplace, but often remain on 'broadcast' far more than they are on 'receive' so don't pick up irritation. Introverts often assume that their naturally closed down state is interpreted as being a private, reflective person, when sometimes their colleagues read them as aloof and unengaged.

Adopting resilient strategies may convince you that the only person you need to worry about is yourself. In most working situations the hardest work is around relationships, which are built, shaped, and damaged by gaps in self-perception. You may think you're a comic genius, but if people dodge out of the way when they see you coming it might be time to tone down your routine.

# Get better at organizational politics

> 'Employees hate meetings because they reveal that self-promotion, sycophancy, dissimulation and constantly talking nonsense in a loud confident voice are more impressive than merely being good at the job – and it is depressing to lack these skills but even more depressing to discover oneself using them.'
> Michael Foley

> 'Companies aren't families. They're battlefields in a civil war.'
> Charles Duhigg

> 'The early bird gets the worm, but the second mouse gets the cheese.' Willie Nelson

> 'Competition brings out the best in products and the worst in people.' David Sarnoff

> 'By working faithfully eight hours a day, you may eventually get to be a boss and work twelve hours a day.' Robert Frost

Robert Half International published a report on office politics in 2012. Although most respondents said they were not actively involved in office politics, 56% indicated that they had seen 'political manoeuvrings' in the workplace. These included gossip, flattering the boss to gain favour, sabotaging co-workers, and taking credit for others' work.

To those who enjoy organizational politics, it's about competition, getting ahead, winning. To those who lose out, it's about deception, manoeuvring, and an unhealthy interest in making sure others don't succeed. Politics at work causes conflict, a lack of shared goals, and ultimately results in cynicism.

A management consultant was invited in to work with the board of a fashion company. The directors identified a key problem they wanted to solve: excessive organizational politics. The consultant's feedback was blunt and direct: you are the organization. 'Political' behaviour often starts at the highest level, and if leaders tolerate it or are complicit with it, it will multiply. Start by being aware of the key influencers in your organization, and work out how they get their results. Draw your line in the sand. Before the pressure is turned on, be clear about how far you are prepared to go to win, and think also about consequences. Identify politics-free teams and projects; some managers believe in co-operation rather than division. Get them on your side, and follow their strategies.

Feeling victimized by office politics is a sure-fire way to damaged resilience. You feel undermined, sidelined, even that your work is being sabotaged by delays or misinformation. You may be receiving what is described in diplomatic circles as 'all assistance short of actual help'.

How far you're complicit in destructive workplace behaviours is going to have an impact on long-term relationships. Political 'players' often have a very short-term perspective, but you have to have a good memory to tell lies at work. Never believe that it's just the way things are – manipulative behaviours are about seeking out weaknesses and creating victims. If you tacitly agree to play dirty, someone will get hurt, and it's just as likely to be a customer as a colleague.

## DON'T TAKE SIDES

In office politics, it's common to have opposing factions, usually linked to two or more individuals who are building power bases. While silos are being defended and empires built, individuals can easily be chewed up or sidelined.

You might believe that the simplest method is to side with the strongest party. Doing that, however, means you play by house rules. Soon you'll be withholding vital information and telling half-truths. How long before you begin to sabotage the 'opposition' actively? Be particularly careful of attempts to manipulate your behaviour. The big problem of engaging, even passively, in office politics is that you only win by losing – by losing integrity, friends, losing focus on why you're in work. Very few people hit retirement wishing they had been more cunning at work; many wish they had more real friends.

If sides are drawn up, be careful not to give allegiance for tribal reasons. If you are going to lend your energy to a group of people, do so because their goals are the most visibly aligned to those of the organization. As far as possible, be completely even-handed about how you share information.

## AVOID DAMAGING YOUR INTEGRITY

Many business writers argue that 'political' skills are vital for building a successful career, and you're unlikely to succeed because of job performance alone. What this recognizes is that successful performers are good at decoding organizations, influencing key people, and building strategic relationships. When you match real insights into the needs of your employer with an ability to persuade, enlist support and get results from other people, everyone benefits. The false assumption is often that you have to manipulate people to take them in your preferred direction.

The negative aspects of playing politics at work are outlined above. Identify the damage caused by playing politics: the deals that are missed, the talent that leaves the organization.

There are of course positives arising from relationships of understanding and trust. Being politically aware is not about telling lies to advance, or ensuring that colleagues fail. It is always about building relationships, inside and outside your organization. It often means choosing your battles carefully, and not getting into conflict over things that don't matter. In addition it requires an ability to map out where you are likely to find people who can give you what you need, whether that's information, support, or someone to champion your cause. At times this will involve sharing your successes with others, but there are ways of doing this which can sound more like information sharing than trumpet blowing.

Do what you say you will do. This builds trust far more robustly than any promise you give.

## WATCH YOUR BACK

When underhand rules of work apply, the results are only indirectly about products or systems; the first effect is to create losers. It's raw playground stuff: 'we don't want you on our team', and no less subtle than other forms of psychological bullying.

Since manipulative behaviour is often prompted by fear, check if you are treading on someone else's toes. Are you in somebody's way? Many honest, diligent people just don't see the knife aimed at their back, so try to team up with colleagues who have better 'radar' than you.

Although you're not the first or the last person to be treated this way, don't make the mistake of believing that the best thing is to lie low and hope the problem will go away. Manipulative behaviour coerces, and the thing it coerces most effectively is silence. Find a mentor to tell you how far you are part of the problem, but do bring the issue to the attention of anyone who can do something about it.

If you have to deal with difficult behaviours, name and respond to the behaviour rather than criticizing the person. Saying 'I felt uncomfortable when you criticized my presentation' is far less challenging than 'you're always negative'.

Don't beat yourself up because you're not good at handling office politics – few people can do so without compromising personal integrity. If you can't find a way a way through, look for a way out, or at least across to another team.

### Putting it all together

A colleague has a work scoring system. Every time his employer requires him to do something unacceptable, he issues an imaginary red card. When the third red card comes out, he looks for a new role.

Coercive, manipulative and victimizing behaviours look on the surface like forms of strength; it's easy to be seduced into thinking that the only way to build tough-mindedness is to 'do unto others before they do you'. Allowing or complying with destructive behaviour ultimately means putting small-mindedness before co-operation, and turning a blind eye to the way people are treated.

Workplace values are shaped by role models. Keep integrity as your surprise card; stick to your principles, and don't dilute them. Honest, non-manipulative styles can draw out positive behaviours from others – it has to start somewhere, so why shouldn't it start with you? Co-operate rather than compete. Be honest with yourself: how far does your success depend on edging someone else towards failure? Avoid making critical remarks about colleagues: you never know how your words will be passed on. Find something positive to say or keep your peace.

Move out of cynical groups, who achieve less, because they start from the position that every new idea has been tried before. If you have something better to offer than your colleagues, put the focus on your offer rather than on ways of making yourself look better than others.

Be consistent. It's no use having integrity one day and being a conniving manipulator the next.

# (29) Learn to say 'no' better

> *'A "No" uttered from the deepest conviction is better than a "Yes" merely uttered to please, or worse, to avoid trouble.'*
> Mahatma Gandhi

> *'Hell isn't merely paved with good intentions; it's walled and roofed with them. Yes, and furnished too.'* Aldous Huxley

> *'Learn to say 'no' to the good so you can say 'yes' to the best.'*
> John C. Maxwell

> *'Look into your own heart, discover what it is that gives you pain and then refuse, under any circumstance whatsoever, to inflict that pain on anybody else.'* Karen Armstrong

> *'Charm is a way of getting the answer yes without asking a clear question.'* Albert Camus

Managers paid to make decisions under pressure don't just do so about strategy, budgets and problem solving; they make quick decisions about people, too. One of the most common is deciding whether a member of staff is onside or offside, the right or wrong kind of person. You might be described as being 'on message', a 'team player', or 'solid'. You might, however, be described as 'not on the same page' as your colleagues, or in even more negative terms such as 'a waste of space'.

One feature of the business world that people don't always understand is that managers don't spend much time making that decision. Key influencers who make a big difference to your future often see contributions in fairly black and white terms – you're either in, or you're on your way out. How you are seen will have a direct impact on how you are treated. It dictates the extent to which you are set up to fail (see Chapter 17), or encouraged. Either scenario can have a big impact on your resilience.

Senior managers watch to see how employees play the 'yes/no' game – whether you say 'yes' to a new idea, to change, to a request for help, for work which isn't strictly in your job description. A short 'no' can close down your future fast. Saying 'yes' begrudgingly, half completing a task or handing it back untouched has equally negative connotations.

Saying 'yes' too easily threatens resilience. Doing so means taking on tasks without thinking carefully about how they will impact on your current workload. What are the chances that you will be successful? What happens if you're not – and what happens to everything else on your 'to do' list?

## SAY 'NO' WITHOUT SOUNDING LIKE YOU'RE SAYING IT

Think about initial reactions. Your first response to a request may be to frown or shake your head. No matter what you say next, your body language has slammed a door shut.

Work on tone. Some people are really good at giving a very clear 'no' that sounds almost like a 'yes'. How do they do it? Charm plays a big part, which is really about making whatever you say sound warm and helpful. Work in your personal style, but starting with 'I can see you've got a problem there', or 'thank you for thinking of me', can be effective openers.

One way to say 'no' gently is to ask for time. Saying 'Can I think it through and get back to you tomorrow?' may be enough to find the task another home – and you haven't said 'no'. You might respond positively but indicate that the request comes at a bad time. Try passing a task back with added value: 'I wish I had the time to deal with this. When you do find someone who can take it on, can I recommend that you look at this earlier project for some tips?'.

## SAY 'YES, IF ...'

If saying 'yes' quickly leads to more work than you can handle, try 'yes, if'. It's a 'yes', so marks you down as co-operative, but it has a tail.

- Yes, if I can have more time than you're anticipating.
- Yes, if I can negotiate some extra resources or support.
- Yes, if you can brief me on the details.
- Yes, if I can talk to someone who has done this before.
- Yes, if I can check in with you in a week or so to ensure that I am delivering what you want.
- Yes, if I can work from home.
- Yes, if you can relieve me of another commitment.

The last trading point can be tricky to pull off, but it's often realistic to say 'if I do X, Y can't happen'. As with all these responses, if your response sounds more like 'I'm really keen to do this, but ...' and less like a blocking manoeuvre, the more you are strengthening your work reputation. The alternatives, including a blunt 'no', saying 'yes' but whingeing, or taking on tasks that you never complete, are likely to get you into difficult territory.

## GET MORE MILEAGE OUT OF SAYING 'YES'

You may be in a role where you have little influence about how and when jobs are delegated to you, and saying 'no' might put your job at risk. However taking on tasks you fail to handle properly can be more risky than an honest conversation about what you can do with the resources available.

If you always have to say a non-negotiable 'yes', say it with a smile. Decision-makers respond to and remember attitude, so accepting work resentfully is counterproductive. So if you're given a difficult task, adopt some of the strategies outlined above, but you can also simply say 'Yes, I'd be really pleased to help you with that. I'm happy to put this document / project on hold, if that's OK with you.'

If the ask is a big ask and all your instincts say that it would be career suicide not to say 'yes', there are still protective strategies available. Agree a timescale, and talk honestly about any snags you might hit. When you hand in the completed task, indicate how long it's taken you, what you've had to put on hold, and who has helped you complete the task. Good feedback to superiors about the real level of difficulty involved helps managers become better delegators and reduces the risk that impossible tasks will be dumped on your desk at zero notice.

## Putting it all together

It's easy to find yourself saying 'yes' if you're a people pleaser, and then end up with way too much on your plate. You may really be saying 'I want you to like me'. Promising the earth and delivering fresh air may achieve the opposite. Manage your initial response to requests for help. Teach yourself to ask for more information rather than giving an instant answer.

If you can't take time to think, at least have some realism about the consequences of saying 'yes'. Learn to manage knee-jerk co-operation, which is habit forming. Ironically, saying 'yes' to everything means you end up doing the tasks no one else wants to do, not the things that develop you.

When managers have decided to delegate tasks they find it irritating to hear 'no'. In their minds the task has already left their desk, and you're putting it back. How you say 'no' matters. Whether you say 'yes' or 'no', make sure that your real message, no matter what outcome is agreed, is that you want to help.

Learn to say 'yes' on your terms, setting and observing boundaries for yourself. At the same time, develop strategies for saying 'no' without damaging relationships or tarnishing your reputation.

Sometimes the answer is to smile and get on with it. If you say yes to major tasks, scope them carefully, which also shows you understand their complexity.

# 30 Pause

**‘** *Time is the great physician.’* Benjamin Disraeli

**‘** *Speak when you are angry and you will make the best speech you will ever regret.’* Ambrose Bierce

**‘** *Don't let the past steal your present.’* Terri Guillemets

**‘** *For every minute you remain angry, you give up sixty seconds of peace of mind.’* Ralph Waldo Emerson

**‘** *Listening is not waiting to talk.’* Scott Ginsberg

Change dominates our life, increasing in speed as every year passes. We are ambivalent about this pace: it's exhilarating as well as frustrating. People complain about being busy and rushed, but for many an overstuffed diary is a secret source of pride, and busyness is equated with good business.

Others know that the resilient mind is a quiet mind. Not all the time, naturally, but there needs to be moments when you pause and take stock. The brain needs variety, rhythm and refreshment as much as the body. Over-activity is one of the most powerful drugs in our society – the legal high of being frenetically busy reinforces a sense that we are irreplaceable.

There are people who, even when dealing with the gravest personal situations, perhaps sitting in a hospital waiting for news of a seriously ill relative, still find time to check their phone for incoming emails. The phenomenon of working from the beach, checking and answering messages, is widely known. Many professionals go into work on a Sunday morning because it's quiet. We seem to have moved on entirely from the 1990s preoccupation with life-work balance into uncharted territory of over-engagement.

You may have to make an effort to take time to think. One way is to choose to press the 'pause' button. There are a wide range of strategies for doing so, from meditation to taking 30 seconds between tasks to gather yourself. The important thing is to choose to pause, regularly. Pausing might include a review of past events (see Chapter 32).

Don't fall into the trap of thinking that pausing is for wimps and is a sign of indecisiveness. Yes, we can prevaricate and at times think too much, but most of the time we merely react rather than reflecting. Looking at a situation takes more than a glance. Listening to what people have to say to you requires more than the occasional sound bite. Understanding may sometimes come in a flash, but usually it takes time to absorb what's really going on and to process what you think about it.

# ALLOW DIFFICULT TEXT TO MULL OVERNIGHT

As Chapter 9 reveals, although it's useful to write things down when you feel anxious, it pays to wait several hours before pressing 'send'. It's best not to write any document emotionally, unless it's a love letter. Whether it's a letter of resignation, a demand, a caustic reply or even a job application, finalizing it when you're tired, unhappy or feeling low is always a bad idea.

Allow yourself time to reflect with any document which is vaguely difficult – in terms of tone, content, intention, impact, or potential consequences. 24 hours will do fine. It's the old advice 'sleep on it'. Get a good night's sleep and read the text again, and you may wonder who wrote it. Review, redraft, and if time allows sit on it a while longer. It's worth letting a complicated or difficult email message rest unsent in your outbox for half a day (and this is a good way of letting your brain catch up to remind you of the things you forgot, such as attachments).

With some difficult communications you will discover that they should stay in a special folder in your filing cabinet, described below.

## CREATE A SIN BIN

Bouncing back from problem circumstances requires a range of strategies, and one of them is discretion. Create a sin bin: a folder in your filing cabinet at home for important letters and emails you will never send. This should not be an electronic folder on your laptop or PC; this stuff is far too sensitive. In that folder will be hard copies of letters you write just to get things out of your system. These letters might be caustic, abusive, angry, bitter – you name it – any part of the gamut of emotions. You can write or say anything you like, because this correspondence isn't going anywhere. It's pure therapy.

The list of things you might keep in this folder is boundless: references, appraisal reports, resignation letters, letters to newspapers, draft Tweets or Facebook announcements. Write what you like as long as you obey three rules:

1. Don't send them anywhere. Don't consider sending even an edited version of a hostile message unless you have reflected on it objectively for several days.
2. Don't keep electronic copies. Print them out and then delete the electronic version. It's all too easy to send things by mistake, and you don't want the wrong things lying around on your laptop at work.
3. If the time comes when the issue no longer bothers you (and you can't see why you got so upset), rejoice that the moment is past, and shred the document.

## REMEMBER THAT MOST STATES ARE TEMPORARY

Look back at times when you felt really anxious or worried by a situation. You probably had physical reactions, too, like sleeplessness or digestion problems. Picture what you were like at the moment of greatest anxiety. Now remember what you were like when this state had largely passed. How long did that take? Seven days, five days, perhaps even just 48 hours.

In locked-in emotional states we believe something is 'forever', or at least that the feeling will never go away. For most contexts, the emotional response will change far more quickly than we realize. You may simply feel differently in the morning, see new solutions, or at least the possibility of a Plan B. Alternatively distractions come along; new concerns often crowd out the old. It's almost like a physiological reaction – if your skin itches, applying heat or cold can mask one sensation with another. The brain tends not to accumulate multiple concerns but focuses on what presents itself now. That focus is what makes the issue seem big and permanent.

Learn to question the absolutes you tell yourself when you're at a low ebb. One problem may be tough to resolve, but your 2 a.m. brain (see Chapter 9) says 'I'm always indecisive'. You may regret one action but your brain says 'I'm always putting my foot in it'. Watch out for the nagging feeling of unease that lingers if something small has gone wrong – identify it and deal with it.

### Putting it all together

Take a few seconds at the end of a task before beginning the next one. Some like to do this by clearing their desks, others by closing down all open computer programs.

Pausing can also be about gaps between sentences. At Quaker meetings, and sometimes in Action Learning Sets, a valued discipline is not to interrupt, and to allow a period of silence to follow any spoken contribution. Try taking a moment to pause before speaking, even in a meeting, so that your answer comes from a less cluttered brain.

The danger of the modern world is that instant responses are expected, and it's also vaguely tempting to respond vigorously while you feel most agitated – the communication equivalent of banging the door when storming out of a room.

Pausing can help you to build better relationships. Before picking up the phone, take 30 seconds to imagine the face of the person you are ringing. When replying to an email, try typing the first name of the person you are replying to in full, as in 'Dear Eileen', rather than just using an initial or beginning the message without mentioning the recipient's name. Hold that person in your thoughts for a second or two; it will improve the tone of what you write.

Pause most when difficult things come along, even if they are also exciting. If someone asks you to do something problematic, take at least a few moments before you give any kind of answer, and ideally reflect overnight.

# Seek out calm space

> ❝ 'True silence is the rest of the mind, and is to the spirit what sleep is to the body, nourishment and refreshment.' William Penn

> ❝ 'Like water, we are truest to our nature in repose.' Cyril Connolly

> ❝ 'Concentration is the ability to think about absolutely nothing when it is absolutely necessary.' Ray Knight

> ❝ 'Most people are about as happy as they make up their minds to be.' Abraham Lincoln

> ❝ 'To be yourself in a world that is constantly trying to make you something else is the greatest accomplishment.'
> Ralph Waldo Emerson

When things tip you off balance the natural instinct is to respond, to correct things through action. Often this gets you into trouble. As Chapter 9 shows, the email you fire off in the middle of the night never represents a full set of feelings, just one trigger response.

We live in an age which demands that information is processed at lightning speed and problems are addressed immediately. This can mean that you act first and reflect later – the 'shoot, ready, aim' school of preparation.

In terms of building resilience, this may not be the best approach. You may end up spending a great deal of time undoing the damage done by a response rooted in anger or resentment, or regretting moving too soon out of confusion or frustration.

Important decisions made under pressure may not be of the best quality, particularly unacknowledged emotional pressure.

Finding calm space allows you to step back from high-speed input-and-response living. This can be physical space which encourages quietness and reflection, for example a room in your home which is free of electronic screens and devices and allows you to think, read, and daydream. It may be your favourite outdoor spot.

You can also actively create and protect calm time. We often make the mistake of thinking that any time away from work is fit for purpose, but it isn't. Even if you take a long weekend you will have the stress of getting to and from your destination, and it may take you more than 24 hours to unwind after a busy week. If some of that weekend time is spent checking email and voicemail messages, you're back in work mode.

If you have some thinking to do, leisure time sometimes isn't enough. There is a difference between taking a few days off and a proper, well-structured withdrawal. This is something closer to a retreat: a time when you are free from the summoning of telephones, screens, even sometimes family pressures. It may sound a luxury or dream, but it can be done even on a budget.

## DON'T WORK ON EVERY JOURNEY

On any commuter or intercity train you will see people engaged in a wide range of habitual activities. They are usually in that mode within five minutes of departure. Some immediately switch on a laptop; others pick up their phones. Those travelling in company chat to neighbours. Others are knitting, reading. Some are looking out of the window.

It's tempting to think of travel time as being 'useful' for work. It's harder to be interrupted, and a good excuse to silence your phone and get on with a task. It seems a good time to read or write detailed documents.

Look again at those people who are 'just' staring out of the window. Don't assume it's because they couldn't find something to read. They may be enjoying the experience, looking at what the world presents, seeing how the seasons change the landscape. They may be mulling things over, perhaps even unconsciously. It's interesting how many problems are solved by not thinking about them, but only if your mind is relatively still.

Many successful executives don't take work with them on long flights or train journeys. They listen to music, daydream, or read a novel, because they know that by decluttering and freeing up their creative mind they will be able to do some longer term thinking, and that sometimes this happens under the surface while apparently you're not thinking at all.

## CLEAR THE DECKS

We all have our excuses for not finding calm space and time. The usual is the idea that we are too busy. How much activity is really about going round in circles? Often this about doing the next thing, not the right thing.

Simplify and declutter. This might be about your diary, but it could also be about your working space. Distraction is a great way of allowing yourself to fragment your attention in many directions at once. Don't clutter your desk with documents that you have parked because they are vaguely interesting – you will repeatedly pick them up and glance over them, but rarely read them in depth.

If you can find calm time, you may also find it helpful to secure a calm space. This may be a bench in the park, but that relies on finding a quiet time of day, and hoping that someone else isn't occupying your favourite spot. It's better to have some part of your home which is a very simple, calm space. Choose a room with good natural light, a room where there are no screens or electronic noises. Take some time. Meditate, think if you like, or just sit. It will be far more productive than you imagine.

## DON'T DO SOMETHING, JUST SIT THERE

Take a moment. You don't need to join a meditation class to start to experience a bit of stillness.

One simple discipline is to stop when you have completed a task. This is easier if you are someone who resists multi-tasking, but most people overwork by trying to fit overlapping activities into the working day. Even if the only thing you do on finishing a task is to close down a folder on your computer, take a moment. Pause (see Chapter 30).

Resist the temptation to move directly onto the next thing. Deep, slow breathing is always helpful here as it will always have a calming effect. Breathe in slowly and gently, taking longer than you would normally, and release your breath slowly. Keep your mouth half closed as you breathe out so it takes longer to expel the air. Try doing this as slowly as you can, seeing how long you can make a quiet 'ffff' or 'ssss' sound (if there's no one nearby to disturb). Or just close your eyes, allow your lungs to empty as gently as possible, mentally sounding the word 'pause' or 'still' on every out breath.

There are computer programs available which remind desk workers to change posture regularly during the working day to avoid fatigue and muscle strain. You can use one, or a timer, or the 'end of task' rule, to take a quiet pause, allowing one activity to rest before picking up the next.

## Putting it all together

It's curious how many of us run daily fantasies about having time to reflect or relax, yet rarely choose to do so. You choose how much of your week to be obsessed by work, and how much time you will give to other things. We blame external factors – work pressures, deadlines, the 24-hour economy – but don't create calm space and time.

Taking time out isn't self-indulgence; it reveals how much of the activity that dominates your life makes sense. It's easy to look and feel busy without having much impact; a review of how much time you actually spend being productive can be a really important step towards success.

Next time you have a long journey, spend some of it just thinking. It may look and feel like staring out of the window, but your subconscious has a much bigger role to play than you might imagine. Allowing things to mull quietly in the background can produce amazing results, and the first idea that you come up with under pressure might not be the best.

Finding calm isn't just for introverts or deep thinkers. Extroverts need it more than anyone else, because sitting quietly and not voicing your thoughts to someone else doesn't come naturally to the kind of people who only understand what they think when they are saying it. But even for the most garrulous or active, small moments of pausing provide big leverage: you make fewer mistakes, have better focus, and see what matters.

# 32 Think differently about the ups and downs

❝ *'There is no black-and-white situation. It's all part of life. Highs, lows, middles.'* Van Morrison

❝ *'The one thing I've learned in the last ten years is that successful artists don't get paid to write and sing songs, they get paid for the psychological roller coaster they're going to have to ride. That's the hard work.'* Enrique Iglesias

❝ *'One of the best protections against disappointment is to have a lot going on.'* Alain de Botton

❝ *If you can meet with triumph and disaster And treat those two imposters just the same'* Rudyard Kipling, 'If'

❝ *'I choose the great roles, and if none of these come, I choose the mediocre ones, and if they don't come, I choose the ones that pay the rent.'* Michael Caine

Life has its ups and downs, some minor, some major. Resilience is about how you cope with the low points. Chapter 2 looks at ways of reframing failure, but this chapter invites you to think about how you respond to the cycle of lows and highs in your working life.

Whether you notice either is very much a reflection of personality. Psychologists currently suggest there are a small group of hard-wired traits, known as the 'Big Five', and one of these is characterized as emotional stability or volatility. This scale records how much you are affected by life's disappointments.

A small part of the population seems virtually immune from the effects of criticism, rejection and even direct attacks on their personality. However the problem with these types is that they are relatively difficult to get motivated – they don't get excited very much by anything, positive or negative.

Most people in any sample group understandably agree that they feel affected by direct personal criticism. If your boss carpets you in a meeting, especially in front of junior staff, that may lower your energy and commitment levels for several days. Some find any form of rejection hard to deal with; for example, being turned down after a job interview.

Further along the scale you find colleagues who feel bruised by the slightest brush-off or implied criticism. They interpret the fact that someone hasn't return a phone call as 'this person doesn't want to speak to me'. They often read the most negative interpretation into events, for example if a reply is delayed, they assume the answer will be disappointing.

The key issue here is not so much how strongly people react, but how long it takes them to revert to normal working levels of confidence. We're all knocked back a little if our best ideas are trashed in a meeting, but some people recover in minutes, others take days or weeks. Being made redundant has no impact on the confidence of some; others take a while to bounce back; some never regain their former confidence.

## DON'T GET CARRIED AWAY WITH YOURSELF

It's great when a plan comes together, you win over a customer, secure a deal, complete a challenging project, or think of a brilliant idea. There are also two dangers in success moments like this. The first danger is that you underrate your personal contribution, and quickly forget the achievement. As resilience is chipped away, so is your databank of evidence: you quickly forget how well you've done in the past.

The second is almost the opposite problem: believing that you are entirely responsible for every success you have ever achieved. The chances are that you won't have got there unassisted: colleagues will have advised, provided key information and helped you avoid bear traps along the way. You may be building on people in the past who have taught you, inspired you, or people whose ideas you have developed or (to be blunt) 'borrowed'. As Isaac Newton said, if we see further it is because we stand on the shoulders of giants.

Success spices up a CV. However if you openly acknowledge the contributions made by others, this builds working communities. In pragmatic terms, you will generally find fewer colleagues interested in competing with you aggressively if you are honest and generous about allocating praise for shared contributions, yet slow to blame if things didn't come off as expected.

## TIME CRITICAL DECISIONS WISELY

Emotional gravity can shift self-confidence quickly. If you make decisions at a high point they may be over-confident; sometimes no bad thing, unless you have an unrealistic sense of your own capabilities. A reality check always helps, particularly if you are about to take on something which is going to stretch you to breaking point.

It's more common to make poor decisions when confidence has dipped. Such decisions are often motivated by an inner desire to escape. If you've just had a very negative appraisal meeting it may be tempting to apply for a new job, but it's almost certainly the worst time to present yourself to alternative employers. If you've just lost a big contract that's a bad time to be making a decision about your future, or indeed anything other than how you ensure you don't lose the next one.

What happens of course is that you're allowing a bruised and damaged temporary mindset to take control of decision-making. Good decisions are made when a calmer person is at the helm.

## SEE UP AND DOWN AS ALL THE SAME

St Ignatius gave his sixteenth-century followers a spiritual exercise featuring consolation and desolation. Consolation was a state of feeling that life couldn't get much better. Desolation was defined by St Ignatius as the 'darkness of the soul, turmoil of the mind, inclination to low and earthly things, restlessness resulting from many disturbances and temptations which lead to loss of faith, loss of hope, and loss of love' (Anthony Mottola, *The Spiritual Exercises of St Ignatius*, Image Books, 1964).

The principles here are useful today. Notice how far you see things in terms of highs and lows. Some of us oscillate rapidly between these two states, boosted by praise or attention, struck low when we are criticized or ignored.

Desolation and consolation are extremes for a reason: neither of them last, and both are about the way we react emotionally rather than the events themselves. St Ignatius asked followers to observe these states objectively and not to confuse them with a deeper-held sense of their identity. When in desolation, he advised, stay the course, don't make changes but stick by the resolutions you made when your mind was unaffected by disappointment. Perseverance is important, but so is the self-discipline not to make new decisions based on emotional triggers.

Equally, when things are going well, learn to 'bank' moments of elation. Remember what it feels like to be respected, admired, a winner. Don't get too carried away with the sensation of being a success – these things don't last long – but do store away the memory of what it feels like to be at the top of your game, otherwise you will easily convince yourself that down is real and up is a false memory.

Remember, most of all, as someone once said 'it pays to make space in your life for disappointment' – it's going to happen sometime.

### Putting it all together

We need new ways to think about the top and bottom of the roller coaster. We might start by learning to see both triumph and disaster as Kipling's 'two imposters' – both are transient and give illusory, precarious pictures of ourselves. Learning that neither success nor failure shapes us forever is a necessary piece of resilient wisdom.

If your emotional life feels like it follows the shape of a sine wave – up and down several times during the course of one working day – look carefully at how you make decisions, particularly those you make when you're feeling emotionally bruised. Explore these feelings carefully, noting what it takes to trigger them. Perhaps you can actively avoid situations where these feelings arise. If you can't, learn to monitor them and recognize them as passing responses that disappear as quickly as they arise.

Think long term: see how frequently these emotional ups and downs come along. If you recognize that your emotional state oscillates wildly, don't assume it's a flaw. People with this kind of emotional movement are often the most energized and committed. You may also recognize that others around you react the same way, needing rather more encouragement and praise than you currently provide.

When things go well, accept and enjoy the accolades, but don't wrap yourself in them. Sip success, don't gulp it down. When you hit a low point, avoid important decisions. Instead, find support, encouragement, or distraction, and pick up the thought again when you're feeling settled.

# 33 Get over yourself

> 'Humility is not thinking less of yourself, it's thinking of yourself less.' C. S. Lewis

> 'If you are all wrapped up in yourself, you are overdressed.'
> Kate Halverson

> 'I think it's one of the scars in our culture that we have too high an opinion of ourselves. We align ourselves with the angels instead of the higher primates.' Angela Carter

> 'Criticism of others is thus an oblique form of self-commendation. We think we make the picture hang straight on our wall by telling our neighbour that all his pictures are crooked.'
> Fulton J. Sheen

> 'Forgiveness does not change the past, but it does enlarge the future.' Paul Boese

When your resilience is working you're hardly aware of it. When minor abrasions come along you accommodate, adjust, and get on with the next task, often without noticing. It's rather like breathing. You take about 20,000 breaths a day, but as soon as breathing becomes difficult because of atmospheric conditions or a health problem, you're aware of every lungful.

Gaps in your resilience grab your attention. Something seems missing, yet something feels like it is taking over. It feels like a more frightened, damaged person has taken control of the steering. You are responding in ways that feel outside your immediate control. Your reactions start to feel more real than the events which have summoned them. You become as focused on your emotional responses as you are on the problem which has triggered them.

So much is now focused on you. Even if you don't think you are the most important person in the situation, your response mechanisms do. When we are activated by anything ranging from discomfort to fear, our focus switches and narrows to ourselves.

That's understandable in the moment, but it can easily linger. It's possible to make every situation about you. You also spend too much time focused on your own thoughts and feelings. In this self-absorbed state you miss things; you lose focus on how others are thinking and on the bigger picture.

Getting over yourself is also about teaching your brain not to focus on failure. You are most tongue-tied when you worry about speaking, and most likely not to remember something when you worry about forgetting. These are times when it helps to focus on something else – your plan, your audience, whatever is going well.

If you're going to focus on your own feelings, pick some good ones. Try to spend some time each week remembering times when life felt good. Keep a notebook to remember days when you felt thankful, peaceful, amused, optimistic, inspired, or experienced joy, serenity, absorption, or love. You'll discover that this kind of self-focus never holds you back or slows you down.

## HANG ON TO YOUR SENSE OF HUMOUR

Have you noticed how colleagues under unusual pressure become very task-focused and lose their sense of humour? Yet some staff faced with even the most frustrating setbacks will find something to laugh at. What's the difference? Perspective.

Laughing at a situation means stepping out of it for a minute and looking at it as if you were a passing observer. This is not only takes tension out of a situation but also reminds you that you're not the most important character in the most significant event of the year, but just another bit part player in a fairly routine comedy. The ability to create comic distance between yourself and events is powerful antidote to stress. Laughing has also been shown to be helpful in lowering blood pressure and speeding up healing. Humour shapes the strongest relationships, because laughing with someone else affirms that you see things the same way. It's healthy to remember that sometimes people are flippant about the things that matter most to them.

Laughter marks a boundary point between not coping and moving forward. You laugh, shake your head, and wonder why you could have got so hot under the collar about something so trivial. Even relatively off-the-wall humour, as long as others share the joke, can relieve stress.

## DON'T BELIEVE YOU'RE THE STAR OF THE SHOW

If you have elevated yourself to the role of principal actor in your personal movie, this has a number of consequences.

The first characteristic of feeling you're the main actor is that it must be your line next. This comes out as a compulsion to speak, usually defensively.

The second is that you start to believe that every other character on stage is talking to you. So if someone mentions that a team member has let others down, how often do you jump to the conclusion that it's you? Don't put yourself centre stage all the time. Allow a few moments, or more, to let new information sink in. Then after reflection you can decide if the issue really does involves you. Try adopting a default position that if it's about you someone will bring it to your attention quickly enough.

Learn to challenge one all-controlling myth – that you have to do everything. If someone mentions a problem, do you assume that you will have to provide the solution? Regularly trotting out the slogan 'if you want anything doing, do it yourself' is a great way to increase your vulnerability to overwork and errors.

## PLAY

The negative consequence of taking yourself too seriously is having to maintain an aura of success. You threaten your own position by giving the impression that your credibility should be judged by consistent, repeated results: 'you're only as good as your last deal'.

In the world of work there are plenty of people who will set you up to fail (see Chapter 17), so why do it to yourself? If every outcome has to be a win to preserve your reputation, winning loses its flavour. Also you start to enjoy only the finishing line and not the race, the destination rather than the journey. You start to avoid risk and therefore become more conservative and less creative.

If you enjoy the process as well as the outcome, and if learning, failing and trying again starts to intrigue and entertain you, you're starting to re-learn an important activity – play. Turning routine tasks into games can add interest, but the most powerful outcome of playfulness is that it frees your mind up to see new possibilities.

Play allows you to set aside worry about whether what you're doing looks good or is productive. Being experimental is about looking at things with an open mind: genuine exploration rather than going over old ground.

If you play you become absorbed in what you're doing, but not absorbed in yourself. In fact one of the side effects of working in the moment like this is that you stop worrying about problems and about yourself. A great way to get over yourself is to pour yourself into something else that feels worth doing just for the fun of it.

### Putting it all together

Taking yourself too seriously isn't just about being pompous or not seeing weaknesses all too evident to others. It's about putting the spotlight on yourself, believing that all problems require your attention, and feeling you have to speak and act first in any situation.

When you're the protagonist in the drama, the only things that seem important are the things you can see. So you believe that no one is reacting, miss how others feel, or pretend that your colleagues' feelings aren't as important as your own.

You also miss the big picture by being too close to the detail. Humour allows you to step back, but can also improve morale, remove tension, and form a bond between people under pressure.

Trying to sustain a very serious image is too often about concealing weakness and any sense that you might take risks or fail. This is self-defeating in resilience terms – you're forcing others to judge you against the benchmark of repeated success. This pushes out possibilities for anything other than very predictable personal development, because it becomes increasingly risky and 'inappropriate' for you to be playful in the workplace, in terms of either humour or experiment.

Playfulness enables you to make connections between things and with people. Enjoy the journey, not just the destination. Experimentation necessarily involves mistakes, but also provides unexpected discovery and learning.

Not taking yourself too seriously provides a healthy objectivity – you take the time to see yourself as others see you, and put the problem in context.

# 34 Practise gratitude

> 'The object is to keep busy being something … as opposed to doing something. We are all sent here to bring more gratitude, more kindness, more forgiveness and more love into this world. That is too big a job to be accomplished by just a few.'
> Richard Nelson Bolles

> 'Silent gratitude isn't very much use to anyone.' Gertrude Stein

> 'As both a feeling and an awareness, gratitude is a virtue with ethical consequences. When we feel most grateful, it is impossible to be cruel or callous, brutal or indifferent.'
> Marcus Borg

> 'The deepest craving of human nature is the need to be appreciated.' William James

> 'Positive anything is better than negative nothing.' Elbert Hubbard

Careers author Richard Nelson Bolles, quoted above, is a public proponent of gratitude – not just expressing proper thanks to all those people who help us along the way, but also thanking family and friends on a daily basis. Gratitude, like resilience, is not just an aspect of character, although it's obvious that some people are prone to saying 'thank you', and others learn to do so or need reminding from time to time.

An article in the online *Harvard Mental Health Letter* published in November 2001 stated that 'gratitude helps people feel more positive emotions, relish good experiences, improve their health, deal with adversity, and build strong relationships'. Other research suggests that expressions of gratitude lower hostility and increase the chances of reciprocally warm behaviours. What goes around really does come around.

One of the reasons that gratitude is an important part of resilient living is that it reflects a healthy understanding that good things come from outside ourselves. While you can't require others to take responsibility for your well-being, they can make a big contribution.

Most research into the non-financial motivators that help retain talented staff discuss the importance of positive feedback. For example the November 2009 edition of *McKinsey Quarterly* included an article by Dewhurst, Guthridge, and Mohr, 'Motivating People: Getting Beyond Money', which concluded that career satisfaction and retention are likely to increase where people receive 'praise and commendation' from their immediate manager, as well as 'leadership attention'.

In an article titled 'A serving of gratitude may save the day' (*New York Times,* November 2011), John Tierney suggested that cultivating an 'attitude of gratitude' has been 'linked to better health, sounder sleep, less anxiety and depression, higher long-term satisfaction with life and kinder behaviour toward others, including romantic partners'. Tips for expressing gratitude even if you don't feel inclined to do so include keeping a journal listing just five things you feel grateful for during the course of a week. Research conducted by Robert A. Emmons of the University of California suggests that even this minimal level of gratitude measurably improves optimism and happiness, and even helped some groups sleep better. Dr Emmons' summary? 'Count blessings, not sheep'.

## TAKE TIME OUT TO BE GRATEFUL

Ask busy professionals the last time they had a really brilliant day at work, and there's a good chance they will tell you about a time they were thanked properly. This is more than a passing remark: 'thank you' is often social noise that means little. This is a time when someone went out of their way to drop by and say 'thank you', properly and warmly, for your time and trouble. Or perhaps someone sent you an old-fashioned 'thank you' card or letter, a gift, some flowers, or some other appropriate but surprising expression of genuine appreciation.

When someone thanks you properly (you know the difference between real and perfunctory thanks), you remember the event and tell stories about it. If you post someone a proper 'thank you' card (not just expressing thanks, but saying why you are grateful and how the other person has helped you) the recipient may well hang on to it, on a notice board, under the glass of a desk, or in a special file for such messages. Even saying thank you warmly in person can buoy someone up for the rest of a working day.

What's even more powerful is taking the time to express gratitude to people who have made a difference to you over a long period of time. Don't wait for Christmas, a birthday, or an anniversary. Don't wait for a pretext at all: gratitude of this kind is sometimes best coming completely out of the blue. Turning up at someone's front door with a bouquet of flowers or a case of wine completely unannounced is relationship-cementing stuff.

## MAKE SURE YOUR GRATITUDE IS RESPECTED

Think about what people hear when you say 'thank you', particularly if you say it unconvincingly, too often, or in a way that sounds like grovelling. Saying 'thank you' to people who are making your life difficult is even more complicated; it can sound like a request to be walked over (see Chapter 23).

If someone helps you but could have done so quicker, then a simple 'thank you' is probably fine unless the delay is important and repeated. However if someone helps you in such a way that they are passing the buck and handing the problem back to you, gratitude is probably the wrong signal as it could be an invitation to do it again, or it may sound very sarcastic.

Being grateful doesn't mean that you should feel permanently indebted. If it feels like someone's help comes at a cost, be careful about the deal you're accepting, especially if you go overboard with your thanks.

# DON'T OVERDO IT

While saying 'thank you' properly is something that has gone out of fashion, it's still important to be clear about the signals that you send out if you overdo it, thank people inappropriately, or thank people to avoid saying something more difficult.

Saying 'thank you' too often reinforces the idea that you have no idea what you're doing and need help. Consider doing something reciprocal instead – it shows you can take the initiative rather than expressing gratitude in a way that makes you sound helpless and in need of rescue (see Chapter 6).

Don't let yourself fall into the habit of excessive but bland gratitude, especially for small and routine acts of support. It shouts out insincerity, and it makes it harder when you really want to show gratitude. On the other hand, be alert to times when someone has gone the extra mile for you, particularly where this wasn't something you asked for. Failing to notice gifts of time and attention can sour working relationships. Rather than thanking everyone for everything, pick out a few occasions every day for which you're really grateful, and try to really communicate your gratitude, going for quality rather than quantity.

Gratitude can also mask your abilities. It's gracious to thank other people for their contribution to your successes, but not if that means that decision-makers are seriously confused about who made a difference. If you are someone who thanks everyone else and downplays your own contribution, you may be using gratitude to hide low self-esteem.

### Putting it all together

Of all the steps we can take to improve relationships, saying 'thank you' is nearly always the cheapest and easiest. Think of all the people you know who say that their working lives would be improved beyond measure with a bit of appreciative feedback. We know it, but – in organizational terms at least – we don't do it.

Don't underestimate the power of small acts of kindness, and the even greater power of noticing them. On a pragmatic level it shows that you are aware of the contributions of colleagues. On a human level it's a powerful motivational tool that is seriously under-employed. Expressing gratitude is a key ingredient in happiness. Helping others to feel better about themselves helps you feel better about who you are, which inevitably provides several layers of protection against life's less pleasant events.

Gratitude can work in past, present and future. Retrieving positive memories lifts your mood, and attending to the present ensures you don't take good outcomes for granted. Gratitude can be focused on the future maintaining a hopeful and optimistic attitude even when your instincts fight against it.

The concept of resilience can seem inward-looking – a very individual concern. Understanding the important contribution gratitude makes to each person's sense of well-being is a useful reminder that it's not all about you; we cultivate resilience with and through other people, particularly those people who take up some responsibility for our growth and development, even if this is through everyday acts of encouragement.

You don't do resilience alone.

# 35 Cut yourself some slack

> 'If you want to support others you have to stay upright yourself.'
> Peter Høeg

> 'Blame is just a lazy person's way of making sense of chaos.'
> Doug Coupland

> 'Thankfully, persistence is a great substitute for talent.'
> Steve Martin

> 'There comes a time when you look into the mirror and you realize that what you see is all that you will ever be. And then you accept it. Or you kill yourself. Or you stop looking in mirrors.' Tennessee Williams

> 'The curious paradox is that when I accept myself just as I am, then I can change.' Carl R. Rogers

The number one problem for people who review their own behaviours and motivations is – you guessed it – they frequently think too much. Self-checking is useful, but you can do too much of it. You begin to go round in circles of regret. You start to invent things that never happened and give false weighting to the things that did. For example when you remember difficult moments you place more emphasis on what you said than on the event as a whole.

If you occupy the whole picture, there's very little else to look at. Some people always blame others (even if it comes out as 'I blame myself for trusting you to do this properly'); many more people openly blame themselves.

Every working life has its green lights and its stop signs, and the more responsibility you take on, the bigger the road bumps. Sometimes these road bumps include events which flatten confidence and challenge your self-image. Being bullied at work, for example, can easily push you into a cycle of self-doubt, anger and cause you to doubt your own abilities. The same thing is often true where people feel rejected because they are sidelined, turned down for promotion, or made redundant. Anyone working with individuals under these kinds of work stress will affirm how often people beat themselves up for the actions and decisions of others.

Believe it: bad things can easily happen to good people, particularly where organizations are concerned. Organizations frequently require individuals to adopt behaviours they're not terribly proud of. High-pressure work cultures often lead to highly directive, even coercive management styles. When profit margins fade to zero it takes an exceptional employer to treat people with fairness and patience. It's easier to push people harder, and to push people down or out. You may feel terrible because you're pushed into treating other people this way, or because you can't protect your colleagues from business pressures. If so, be clear whether it's you, the organization, or the work culture in general which calls the tune.

## STEP OUTSIDE THE ISSUE

Put the handbrake on if you start sliding downhill into blaming yourself. Even if you have made a genuine mistake, there may be other factors that need addressing apart from your responsibility. Perhaps you lacked information, direction or support? If you find yourself in a situation where your self-esteem has been dragged through the mire, ask 'is any of this about me?'.

It's a cliché that roles rather than people are made redundant. We know that doesn't feel true, but there is some truth in it. Therefore if you talk about being 'let go' when presenting your CV, it's best to talk about the way the organization changed, not about how this change affected you. Similarly, if an organization requires you to do the job of two people with little thanks, remember this is more about working pressures than about your worth as an individual.

Talk things through with someone who can provide a helicopter view of your situation and give you honest feedback about which outcomes are genuinely about you, and which have nothing to do with you at all. Seeing the burdens you don't have to carry is liberating.

## DON'T PLAY THE MARTYR

When someone says to their boss 'I guess it's my fault that ...' or even 'I think I may be the problem here' that's often a disguised plea for reassurance. Your secret hope is that your boss will disagree violently and tell you what a great job you're doing.

The problem of choosing to play the victim game is that it can easily backfire. Think about it: by pointing the finger at yourself repeatedly you're communicating the message that you can't do your job properly. Even if you are doing this ironically, even if you are doing this to gain sympathy and receive a pat on the back, you are still putting yourself down in front of people who matter. If you constantly take the blame for mistakes made by your subordinates, what this may do is subtly communicate the idea that you're not really taking charge.

If you are the kind of person who instinctively runs yourself down, be honest with yourself about the outcome you are seeking. Are you genuinely admitting to failure so that you can learn from the experience? Or is it a back-to-front way of seeking approval? If not approval, perhaps you're moving into victim mode (see Chapter 6).

## TALK IT OUT

How do you break out of the self-blame loop? Stop giving yourself a hard time.

Imagine doing to a good friend what you do to yourself. Imagine ringing them just after their alarm bell goes off in the morning to say 'don't forget that all that stuff last week is your fault'. Imagine texting them at one o'clock in the morning with the same message. How would that friend react if you sent half-hourly emails to interrupt their work flow, perhaps just with that simple message 'you got it wrong, didn't you?'.

No friendship would survive more than 48 hours based on this kind of feedback, but it's what you do to yourself.

Start by accepting that this fact alone is natural. People beat themselves up. They do it a lot, and they are really good at it. They feel guilty for doing it so well. Stop beating yourself up for beating yourself up.

Next, get some perspective. You might achieve some of this by thinking the problem over, but that's usually rather like using a sledgehammer to fill a hole in the road; the more you hammer, the hole just keeps getting bigger. The best results, nearly always, come through talking the situation over with someone who can (1) objectively point to the parts of the situation which are really not about you at all (see above) and (2) remind you of the things you have done well – either in this situation or in the past.

Failing that, invite two friends round to listen to you beat yourself up for an hour. That's it, one hour. After that, brew up or open a bottle and – without slipping back – talk about only positives such as your strengths and where they might take you.

### Putting it all together

Self-deprecation is almost a national characteristic in the UK where we are naturally suspicious of praise. However when people repeatedly put fault at their own door two things happen. Firstly, they believe their own dark picture, and second, others start to believe it too.

Conscientious working professionals self-check all the time. It's an important way of monitoring your impact on others and making sure you aren't treading on too many toes. Reflecting before and after difficult situations enables you to learn far more from them.

Ultimately, it's about adapting your natural working style. Some people never self-check or reflect on their own performance, and yet (perhaps because of this blind spot) can sometimes rise to the highest rungs of the ladder. Others examine themselves too long and too deeply and get stuck in analysis paralysis.

Learn the difference between honest self-appraisal and beating yourself up. Self-criticism is uncomfortable, but it's easy – you don't have to work or think hard to see what went wrong in a situation if you always blame yourself. It's also unimaginative and unfruitful: how much do you learn by putting yourself in the role of clown, klutz or victim?

Beating yourself up too much and too often becomes a habit, and tips over into the way others see you, particularly where you express your doubts in front of the wrong people. Falling into the verbal habit of taking the blame for everything, even tongue-in-cheek, can be even more counter-productive.

# 36 Look after yourself better

> **''** *'Give a man health and a course to steer, and he'll never stop to trouble about whether he's happy or not.'* George Bernard Shaw

> **''** *'The first wealth is health.'* Ralph Waldo Emerson

> **''** *'Sorry, there's no magic bullet. You gotta eat healthy and live healthy to be healthy and look healthy. End of story.'*
> Morgan Spurlock

> **''** *'Surgeons can cut out everything except cause.'* Herbert M. Shelton

> **''** *'Be careful about reading health books. You may die of a misprint.'*
> Mark Twain

Health is one of the biggest factors contributing to feeling good about life. In 2012 the UK government continued its project of monitoring well-being. Being employed, particularly if the work is satisfying enough, is an important factor, as is being in a long-term relationship, having supportive friends and family, being a person of faith, and also feeling part of a community. However the most important factor associated with well-being is the way people view their health. Much of the current research into resilience emphasizes the importance of looking after yourself, and this includes body as well as mind.

According to the Office for National Statistics, 'people who reported very bad health had much lower ratings of life satisfaction, feelings that things were worthwhile, levels of happiness and higher ratings of anxiety on average than those who said their health was good'. The report added: 'People's sense of choice and contentment with their situation affects personal well-being'.

If you have long-term limiting health problems you will, unsurprisingly, find it harder to maintain a positive outlook. However, most of us only recognize the dominant role good health plays in well-being when we start to lose it. These two points are more related than you might think. For some people in our society illness and disability are factors over which they have little control. For most of us, our health and how we choose to protect it are matters where we can exercise a great deal of choice.

It's interesting how often we blame external circumstances for our own choices: 'I eat badly because I'm tired' or 'I drink too much because I'm stressed'. Both are familiar scenarios, and there are plenty more. What we're really doing, of course, is finding new ways of saying 'it's not my fault'.

Staying fit and well for most of us is about choosing how we spend our time and what we choose as fuel. Caffeine, sugar and alcohol are all widely used props, with clear disadvantages. Over-consumption of all kinds can be a comfort, and yet can also progress into a downhill pattern.

## SLEEP ON IT

In 2011 the National Sleep Foundation reported that 63% of Americans felt that their sleep needs were not met during weekdays. Getting enough sleep is as important to resilience as the strongest pep talk.

In the buzz of our 24/7 economy you might consider sleep an irritating distraction, but sleep isn't just for recharging your physical batteries; other kinds of recovery occur. We think that concentration and conscious effort are required for solving problems, forgetting that the brain processes during sleep. This is why problems seem smaller in the morning, and you wake up with a new idea.

If you are handling difficult decisions, let your sleeping brain have a go at them. Good sleep assists good judgement. Take sleep as seriously as work – each takes up roughly the same amount of time across the decades. Arrange your diary so that you put in times to catch up on sleep. Pick a good night to recharge, but don't expect to do this the night before a stressful presentation.

If sleep evades you, watch out for the combined effects of alcohol and caffeine which are capable of resetting your sleep clock as thoroughly as jet lag. Look at research emerging from sleep lab projects; a sleep diary may help you move towards uninterrupted sleep, as does a dark, cool bedroom free of screens and phones.

## TRY ON NEW HABITS

Health is closely related to consumption. The problem with the things we shouldn't consume too often is that they exert a strong attraction, whether it's the first drink in your hand when you get home in the evening or your mid-afternoon chocolate bar.

If you're trying to change habits like this, look at the things that prompt you. For example research shows that 'No Smoking' signs stimulate the urge to smoke. So, if the first thing you see when you get to the office kitchen is a biscuit tin, there's your next thought. Most diets have only short-term benefits. The problem is that they focus your attention on food.

There seem only two real long-term solutions to weight control: eat less, eat better, and keep fit. It can sometimes help to keep yourself focused and active so your attention is away from food, but the danger is that after working long hours you eat ready meals or fast food. Be aware of what happens when you shop, eat or drink when you're tired.

There seems some evidence that fasting one or two days a week can assist with long-term weight control and is generally good for you. Do it properly by taking advice, and on non-fast days eat well rather than more.

## TREAT YOURSELF LIKE A VIP

Imagine your job was to organize someone's diary, in three-month blocks. Your brief is to strike a balance between productivity and refreshment. You'd carefully include breaks between busy periods. You'd pause before saying 'yes' to invitations which are flattering but dull and unrewarding. You'd also pay more attention to maintaining variety, balancing intellectual jobs with practical tasks. You might say 'after spending all day going through budgets I've arranged for you to spend two hours in your garden'. You'd build in time for exercise and rest rather than leaving these things to chance. You'd do a better job than you manage for yourself.

When we organize these things for ourselves we tend to describe balancing activities as 'treats' or 'me time'. By making them sound selfish we make it easier to push them down the agenda, and also easier to gravitate towards the things that are less healthy. Sadly we use the idea of 'me time' to justify eating or drinking too much, often to the exclusion of anything else. However when you review life as a game of snakes and ladders (see Chapter 32) and think of highlight events, often these were times spent with close family, days you found yourself somewhere beautiful, moments when you learned or tried something new, or times you met stimulating people. Taking time out to do things which feel good for the soul is never a bad idea, and enriches the quality of the work you produce.

### Putting it all together

An important step on the road to improved resilience is a degree of honesty about the life choices we allow to become habits. Depriving yourself of sleep, good food, hydration, breaks between tasks – we make these seem like inevitable consequences, but how many of them really are choices? Getting into the office at 6 a.m. or going in at the weekend may be a one-off tactic, but as a routine pattern will set up long-term problems. If you're really required by somebody else to work punishing hours every week, it's time to have a serious conversation about the best way of giving value. If when you honestly analyse your motives you can see you're doing this to yourself (perhaps to impress, or out of fear), then it's time you looked at the consequences of sticking to this plan in the long term.

Dealing with high-stress situations requires perspective, and that comes from stepping away from the situation and yourself (see Chapter 31 on finding a calm space). Your instinct may be to work longer hours, to work harder, to trade recovery time for overwork at the drop of a hat. Think about the consequences.

Looking after yourself better means remembering that your health really is the biggest factor in personal happiness. It matters a great deal to the people close to you as well. So, every time you review commitments of time and energy, think carefully about what you keep in reserve. You may need it sooner than you think.

# (37) Look at stress differently

66 *'There is no stress in any situation until a person has a stress reaction.'* Al Siebert

66 *'The interpretation of stressful events is more important than the events themselves.'* Richard Lazarus

66 *'A "good job" can be both practically attractive while still not good enough to devote your entire life to.'* Alain de Botton

66 *'Stress is difficult to define because it is so different for each of us. A good example is afforded by observing passengers on a steep roller coaster ride. Some are hunched down in the back seats, eyes shut, jaws clenched and white knuckled with an iron grip on the retaining bar. They can't wait for the ride in the torture chamber to end so they can get back on solid ground and scamper away. But up front are the wide-eyed thrill seekers, yelling and relishing each steep plunge who race to get on the very next ride. And in between you may find a few with an air of nonchalance that borders on boredom. So, was the roller coaster ride stressful?'*
The American Institute of Stress

66 *'If you're interested in "balancing" work and pleasure, stop trying to balance them. Instead make your work more pleasurable.'* Donald Trump

Modern society changes relentlessly, and we see stress as the consequence. In 1936 Hans Selye used the word 'stressor' to describe external factors exerting psychological pressure, and 'stress' to describe our response. 'Stress' soon became a popular buzzword used to describe a wide range of symptoms. One physician writing in the *British Medical Journal* in 1951 suggested: 'stress in addition to being itself, was also the cause of itself, and the result of itself'; we become stressed by worrying about stress. Most definitions describe stress in terms of the differential between external pressures and our perception of whether we will be able to deal with them.

Stress is therefore a term used to describe how we feel and also what causes it. Symptoms range from irritability to chronic anxiety leading to symptoms such as palpitations and sleeplessness. Stress is a big theme in work, and is perceived as a curse, a fact of life, or something to be consciously avoided. According to psychologist Richard Lazarus, we feel stressed when 'demands exceed the personal and social resources the individual is able to mobilize'.

Why is it that the same stress factors make some people ill and other people thrive? The answer may lie in the fact that we use the word 'stress' negatively. In physics, stress can produce useful energy (pressure increases grip, applying stress to a bow propels the arrow, and a spring put under stress drives a clock mechanism). There are people who not only manage stress well, they derive positive energy from it.

So, are there good stressors and bad stressors? Few people look forward to the stress of having their teeth filled. Intensely stressful experiences such as bereavement can produce ageing effects; world leaders usually look older than their years after leaving office. Some events are pleasurably stressful. There are those who enjoy sitting examinations, others who hate the experience.

Most events we deal with in working life are mid-zone in terms of impact. Stress is all about whether we notice it, how we see it and what we make of it.

## LOOK FOR YOUR OVERLOAD POINT

Stress is an external force which, at first, increases productivity –
a deadline, for example. In their inspiring book *How to Get Ideas*
(Berrett-Koehler, 2003) Jack Foster and Larry Corby recorded a
project where students asked to produce six advertising ideas in
a lunch break produced better results than those given 24 hours
to produce just one idea.

External pressures can reach a point where stimulation starts to
feel oppressive. So, for example, you take on more tasks than you
can handle and perform none of them satisfactorily; you rush and
make mistakes. The point of overload – where efficiency becomes
damage – varies across individuals as much as engines.

Be sensitive to early warning signals, which are sometimes
subtle. Others may see the signs before you do. What do you
watch out for? Learn your own personal stress indicators. Your
symptoms will probably include several of the following:

- Switching impulsively from one task to another.
- Losing focus and starting to make mistakes.
- Exhibiting frustration at obstacles.
- Losing patience, showing irritation at interruptions.
- 'Closing down' and appearing cold.
- Paralysis: freezing and being unable to make a decision
  or take action.
- Anxious or racing thoughts.
- Feeling overwhelmed.
- Blaming other people for your difficulties.
- Turning to food, alcohol or caffeine for comfort or
  support.
- Sleeplessness or lethargy.
- Feeling isolated or unhappy.

## RESPOND DIFFERENTLY, AT LEAST SOME OF THE TIME

You can't avoid stress, but you can reduce it and control
how much it affects you. Relaxation techniques such as yoga,
meditation, and deep breathing help to alleviate everyday stress
and promote feelings of calm and well being.

You can't make a one-off change which makes you react differently under stress. However, human beings are remarkably adaptable and you can learn to react differently to some things, some of the time.

Start with one work event that happens regularly and always presses your buttons. Perhaps it's the weekly phone call from accounts chasing down figures – the call that always comes when you're doing something vital. Or another frustrating meeting. Or perhaps a work colleague triggers irritation. Focus on that one stressor and decide, right now, to react slightly differently. You might choose to anticipate the weekly accounts call by sending your figures ahead of time, or renegotiate the meeting agenda, or work apart from the irritating colleague.

Decide now how you will react next time the stressor comes along. Perhaps just decide to pause before allowing instincts to turn into words. At the same time, look at the situation from the perspective of other people. Finally, ask yourself if any of this stuff matters enough to engage your energies. Learn to observe initial reactions, put them to one side, do the job in hand, and move on.

## DON'T REPEATEDLY FOCUS ON STRESS

Psychologist Mary Steinhardt, conducting research within the Motorola Corporation, discovered that employees who reported that their jobs were stressful turned out to be less resilient than their peers in similar roles who did not report the same stress levels. Those who used problem-solving strategies to deal with their constantly changing work environment were the most resilient. Al Siebert, author of *The Resiliency Advantage* (Berrett-Koehler, 2005) states: 'the least resilient workers are those who experience their jobs as full of stress'.

Those who work on early morning BBC radio often start their working day well before dawn, but their training instructs them never to talk on air about their own tiredness. Their job is not to focus on their own exhaustion, but to cheer up tired commuters who are not in the slightest bit interested in how tired the broadcaster feels.

Avoid the daily litany of talking about how stressed you feel: it actually increases your stress levels. People who complain about having a full diary are simply turning up the heat on themselves. Ask a colleague to rattle a charity tin at you every time you use the word 'stress'. Constantly painting a picture of failure does nothing for your confidence levels. Talking about stress all the time is like telling yourself that you're falling off a cliff edge. Your attention goes into falling rather than flying.

## Putting it all together

Do we work longer hours than previous generations? BBC Radio 4's *A History of Britain in Numbers* confirmed in 2013 that on average we worked 1,600–1,700 hours per year, approximately half the typical hours of a worker in Queen Victoria's reign, but pretty much on a par with normal working hours in the 1940s.

The difference, however, is how much time we give to work mode outside contractual hours, processing and communicating information. Also the way we work is very different. Today we multi-task far more frequently than previous generations. The pressure to absorb new facts, technologies and processes causes intellectual pressures not experienced by any previous generation. Whether you perceive this as challenge, stimulation, pressure, or stress varies considerably.

What is clear is that even healthy challenges can lead to over-commitment, and the resulting stress causes blind spots. Juggling plates is fun, but you will start to break some. Learn to recognize the early warnings that you are starting to act and see the world through the lens of stress.

John F. Kennedy said that the Chinese word for 'crisis' is a combination of two characters: 'danger' and 'opportunity'. This inspiring paradox is widely quoted by motivational speakers. In fact the second character employed has multiple meanings including 'crucial point' and the paradox isn't as neat as claimed. However the mistranslation still speaks to us; risk and crisis can be interpreted, and shaped, in very different directions including confusion or creativity. Dealing with stress is about dealing with ambiguity.

## 38 Find the right support

Think of your work like being on a see-saw. At times the pressures on the other end are light enough for your weight, your personal resources, to keep your end of the see-saw level. The smallest effort will maintain the balance.

Sometimes the force on the other end is hard for you to counterbalance. It may feel like a sudden extra burden has been added, shooting you upwards until you reach a painful, juddering stop while you are stuck, useless and mid-air. At other times movements are hard to control or predict as forces change. Sometimes your muscles are too tired to respond and the thing moves where it wants, with you feeling like an inanimate object.

The see-saw isn't a bad analogy for resilience. Sometimes balance is easy, but at other times you need extra weight on your side. These might be resources, information, or strategies, but – as with the see-saw – the best help is an extra body or two. Recruiting support resets the balance.

Don't fall for the work myth that you're a stronger player if you solve problems unassisted. Those who struggle on alone are really still in conversation, with their inner demons, their 2 a.m. voices (see Chapter 9), or sometimes just listening to the voices of people who present negative pictures.

We're able to work on our own resilience, but more than a few people are gifted at affirming and building resilience in other people. It could simply be that a bit of perspective helps and it's difficult to find your own solutions. There is also something fundamentally positive about any encounter where one person listens, encourages, suggests different ways of reframing a situation, and then helps you draw out a solution.

Actively seeking support is an important learning stage for the resilient mindset. This isn't just about unburdening yourself or talking about what's going on, important as those stages are. It's also about being conscious and honest about what builds up resilience in daily activity and what chips away at it, then allowing your others to help you to help yourself – to discover new strategies and behaviours and to experiment accordingly.

## WORK ON RESILIENCE WITH A COACH

As coaching becomes increasingly common in business life there are now coaches who specialize in resilience, but many coaches work around this theme. A good coach will help you focus on the life or work factors which are diminishing you, and the circumstances and activities which help to build you up.

However it's sometimes helpful to book time with a coach just to discuss resilience as an issue. You might start with the checklist provided in Chapter 1, spending most time on the factors which you have ticked as very important but which you have given low scores.

Focus on these issues with a coach. Describe what you are like when you are feeling resilient, and what you are like when your resilience has taken a hammering. What work contexts work best for you? What feels like going against the grain?

Your coach will help you focus, too, on behaviours and strategies that will help you protect yourself in difficult circumstances. You may be encouraged to try different approaches; for example, being more direct with people where you need their support or encouragement, or striking a better balance between working activities. You will gain greater self-awareness by discussing how both external circumstances and your internal responses can lift or suppress your energy levels.

When you're focusing on ways of delivering more in your job a coach can help you see the difference between adding to your workload and purposeful, effective activity. Being open in discussion about your resilience and how it is shaped will help you find better ways of delivering additional energy without destroying integrity and well-being. Coaches are often very skilled at helping you work through difficult working relationships.

## FIND A MENTOR

The differences between a mentor and a coach are often hard to spot, but often the most important factors are distance, objectivity, and insider knowledge.

A coach who works inside your organization should be distant enough from you to provide some objective distance. Expecting your boss, or other team members, to coach you is probably unwise – they may be contributing to the problems you are trying to solve. If your coach does work for the same organization as you, you need clear agreed guidelines around confidentiality and accountability.

A mentor is rather different. Mentors are generally people who work for the same organization as you, but usually not alongside you. The relationship usually works best if they are more experienced than you and more senior. However the characteristic that makes a really good mentor, apart from good listening and analytical skills, is the ability to decode.

One of the reasons people become sidelined, stuck in a rut or start to create a negative reputation inside an organization is that they have lost (or never achieved) the ability to decode their own organization. They read and hear the words used by senior decision-makers but don't understand them. They find internal processes opaque or mystifying (particularly relating to learning, seeking help, influencing people and achieving advancement).

A good mentor understands the organization better than you do and can help decode it for you so you see new options for change and growth. Skilled mentors can also provide very useful insights which help you see yourself the way others in the organization see you (see Chapter 27).

## CREATE A SUPPORT TRIO

Create your support trio by finding two other people who pass three simple tests. They need to be positive-minded, 'the glass is more than half full' types. The second is that they are genuinely interested in helping the other two people in the trio. The third is that they need to be able to synthesize information from what they hear; the kind of people who are good at summarizing your skills or reminding you what you're good at.

When you get together, make sure it's face to face – this works best if you spend quality time together (a meal and a bottle of wine helps, but meet somewhere discreet enough for you to share confidences). Secondly, make sure all three are present – as soon as it becomes two people it shifts into a coaching or mentoring relationship.

### Putting it all together

In some circles there is still an idea (emphatically more so for men) that asking for help reveals weakness. This is ironic considering how widely organizations value learning and development and coaching which centre on the idea that everyone needs external assistance to help them grow and change.

Rebuilding and maintaining resilience is rarely achieved best from text resources. Most life problems can only properly be addressed through conversation. Sometimes this is the everyday analysing, brain-storming and mending that happens over coffee, lunch or at the end of a meeting. More often we put time aside and ask someone else to share that time, because others hear things in our words that we don't hear for ourselves, and see options and perspectives that are closed books to a troubled brain.

Adding structure and expertise to these conversations takes them into a different realm. Resilience issues are generally too big, too all-consuming, to engage with alone. It's no surprise that factors which increase resilience and well-being include some sense of feeling supported and encouraged, enjoying relationships of trust, having external resources, and being able to solve problems and make decisions – features often provided by coaching or mentoring relationships.

An equally powerful method is to draw upon the combination of emotional support and creative energy provided by a support trio. Something different happens when two people are listening or imagining. Spend time looking at each other's issues, in turn if necessary, and give each other plenty of positive strokes as well as good ideas.

# (39) Help somebody else

❝ *'A man should never be appointed into a managerial position if his vision focuses on people's weaknesses rather than on their strengths.'* Peter Drucker

❝ *'Most great learning happens in groups. Collaboration is the stuff of growth.'* Sir Ken Robinson

❝ *'None of us is as smart as all of us.'* Ken Blanchard

❝ *'The function of freedom is to free someone else.'* Toni Morrison

❝ *'The place to which we are called is where our deep gladness meets the world's deep hunger.'* Frederick Buechner

If resilience is all about looking after ourselves, isn't it all rather selfish? Is there any room for altruism?

Humans co-operate for all kinds of reasons. Some of it is strategic – *I look after you if I you look after me*, described by sociobiologist Robert Trivers as 'reciprocal altruism'. Sometimes you act in anticipation that you will need help in the future. The more spiritually minded wrap this up as karma: generosity is returned as what goes around comes around.

Whatever the truth of that idea, it's also true that doing good things for other people is, quite simply, good for you. Acts of kindness seem, according to most studies on happiness, to lead to a greater sense of well-being.

John Cacioppo, a social psychologist at the University of Chicago, has undertaken extensive research into loneliness. In *Science* in January 2011 Cacioppo revealed how social isolation increases health risks and mortality, and also makes individuals less able to cope with stressful events. We rely on others to help us process difficult experiences and get our act back together.

Clinical psychologist George Bonanno has conducted studies into psychological responses to shock and stress. His results indicate that no matter how severe the trauma, the proportion of people suffering PTSD usually never exceeds a third of the population. Social groups seem to have a kind of core group of people who can continue to act purposefully after life-threatening events including natural disasters. In turn, anything between one-third and two-thirds of the population demonstrate simple resilience, defined by Bonanno as the ability to function 'with a core sense of purpose, meaning and forward momentum' (*The Other Side of Sadness: What the New Science of Bereavement Tells Us About Life After Loss*, Basic Books, 2010).

Bonanno's big question was 'why are we, as a species, designed this way?'. Some argue that this feature is almost like a race memory, ensuring that after disaster there remains a substantial number of people, possibly even a majority, to take care of those who are deeply affected or disabled by events. Some of us are better equipped to survive, but we're given that ability in order to help the whole tribe to recover.

## DO SOMETHING BECAUSE IT NEEDS DOING

Theologian and novelist Frederick Buechner is famous for his definition of vocation, quoted at the beginning of this chapter. It suggests that meaningful work is about balance: 'the place to which we are called is where our deep gladness meets the world's deep hunger' (*Wishful Thinking: A Seeker's ABC*, Harper Collins, 1993). For Buechner innate talents seek to find a match to pressing needs. It doesn't take great sensitivity or investigative powers to spot the world's 'deep hunger'; apart from those who share our planet who will go hungry today, we're surrounded by emotional and spiritual hunger of all kinds.

Responding to need is sometimes immediate and instinctive. There are times when we have to set boundaries around how quickly we can help and how much time we can give. Do something because you know it works — both for the person you're helping and for you, because a key building block in resilience is a sense that what you do with your time makes a difference in the world, and (for whatever reason) self-effacing acts of kindness really do make you happier.

## PASS ON YOUR EXPERIENCE IN SMALL CHUNKS

If you're going to mentor someone it's tempting to pick winners — rising stars who, when they take off, you can claim as success stories. However the people who need your skills and wisdom most are probably stuck, or in difficulty.

Passing on your experience isn't, usually, about telling your story. If you're helping someone else look at an issue it's easy to make the solution sound simple, just as long as your colleague does the same things you have done. That one-size-fits all approach is generally unsuccessful. This approach puts far too much emphasis on your experience, your story, and what works for you. It's true that knowing you have experienced something similar can be encouraging, and can give someone permission to reveal vulnerabilities. It doesn't mean that they want an prefabricated solution.

Your most important role in this situation is to listen, and then offer objective feedback. You may be the first person to suggest that (1) what your colleague has gone through and is feeling right now are difficult to handle and (2) she is doing pretty well under the circumstances — recognition and simple affirmation are powerful.

Be clear about the stage of the conversation. It may be that the story has to be told, reflected on, and told again. You may feel more like a punchbag than a sounding board for a while. At later stages you will probably be talking not so much about solutions as coping mechanisms: 'how are you going to get through the rest of the week?'. Here your own past strategies may be very helpful — not so much answers, but short-term approaches that worked for you and kept you sane. When it comes to potential solutions, however, dip into your past with care – your actions fitted another context and also fitted you. It's far better to keep asking questions looking at possible ways forward as seen through the eyes of the person you're working with.

## GET CLOSER TO THE PEOPLE YOU'RE HELPING

Modern society has no shortage of people pushed to the edges where they easily become forgotten or invisible – individuals with something to offer but sadly let down by educational and work systems.

Look hard at your impulse to help others. What activities do you end up doing as a result of your charitable intentions? Sitting on committees or going to fundraising dinners can certainly help society, but they often leave you disconnected from the real people you want to help.

Fortunately there are hundreds of organizations who can provide you with opportunities to work one-to-one with someone who can benefit from your experience and energy. These opportunities are as wide ranging as the social problems they seek to resolve. You might be working with an adult on basic literacy, helping a 19-year-old to set up her first business, or working with redundant workers in a church job club. The need is enormous, so if your talent is for one-to-one support, don't let charitable organizations always funnel you into work which looks more strategic and professional – do something at the chalk face.

### Putting it all together

Resilience is reinforced amongst those who believe that life has a meaningful purpose. This can arise from personal faith, or can simply mean engaging in activities which have positive effects for individuals or society.

Gifting your time to someone who has resilience problems is more than kindness. It may be a smart way of developing talent, or retaining someone important. It may be a way of releasing energy you don't have any more, allowing someone else to move back into productive work

If you move on from a difficult time in your life you will probably have quite a few people to thank. Sometimes they gave active help, sometimes they just listened. Sometimes (did you notice?) they just gave you some space or kept out of your way for a while. We can do very little of this on our own. Many of the tips and strategies in this book point you towards getting support and encouragement from other people.

Often busy working people have the best skills, the best connections, and the right energy to help those who are struggling. Don't get locked into a trading mentality, only acting where you can call a favour in later, or the karma game, believing that the universe is a simple input-output mechanism. The least important question is 'what do I get out of it?'. The task needs to be done, and if it can be done by you well and you can improve someone's situation in the process, end of discussion.

# 40 Decode people more effectively

> 'You have to master not only the art of listening to your head, you must also master listening to your heart and listening to your gut.' Carly Fiorina

> 'To the man who only has a hammer in the toolkit, every problem looks like a nail.' Abraham Maslow

> 'I've learned that people will forget what you said, people will forget what you did, but people will never forget how you made them feel.' Maya Angelou

> 'Nobody realizes that some people expend tremendous energy merely to be normal.' Albert Camus

> 'The problem with the world is that the intelligent people are full of doubts, while the stupid ones are full of confidence.' Charles Bukowski

How good is your people 'radar' – your ability to pick up what people are thinking before they use words? Others have a less effective radar and see emotional responses only when they are very visible. Some have no radar at all and neither notice nor value emotional responses.

Emotional intelligence is a term developed in the 1980s and popularized by a range of writers including Peter Salovey and Daniel Goleman. The term Emotional Quotient (EQ) also has some currency. *Harvard Business Review* proclaimed emotional intelligence as 'a ground-breaking, paradigm-shattering idea'.

The model of emotional intelligence suggests that we have a range of abilities: to observe our own emotions, to harness and draw upon them, to understand them in ourselves and others, and to manage them. People with high EQ often show an enhanced ability to understand how emotions are expressed, how they vary, and how they evolve over time.

In his book *Working With Emotional Intelligence* (Bloomsbury, 1999), Daniel Goleman suggests that self-awareness in emotional intelligence (EI) terms is 'the ability to know one's emotions, strengths, weaknesses, drives, values and goals and recognize their impact on others while using gut feelings to guide decisions'. Goleman cites research undertaken at Johnson & Johnson indicating that staff identified at mid-career as having high leadership potential demonstrated stronger EI competencies than their less-promising peers.

One advantage is that you get early indications of what might go wrong. So if someone says 'I agree' in a meeting, your instincts may tell you that they actually mean the exact opposite. Sensing and interpreting body language can often give you a prompt heads-up on what people are thinking, even if they are making all the right noises.

Emotional intelligence provides insights in situations ranging from negotiation to public speaking, but it requires an important commitment: your willingness to know yourself better, understand people more often, and use what you learn to modify your behaviours. Better people radar also provides a good early warning system of human reactions that are likely to push you off-balance and damage your resilience.

## DON'T CONFUSE FEELINGS WITH THINKING

We often confuse thinking and feeling, sometimes for effect. You support an idea because you like the author, not because it will work. You may find an idea frightening, but you'll tell people it lacks rigour. If you're discussing a difficult issue, slow things down to let people express feelings. Ask everyone to speak. If someone tells you to support an idea but you're not convinced, ask them to describe the down side. Try asking questions on more than one level. You could, for example, say 'before we look at the pros and cons, let's all talk honestly about our gut reactions to this'. Get people to declare if their response is based on gut feeling, showing that it's valued. Then ask them to put feelings aside and focus on ways forward, and the consequences of both action and inaction. .

If a team is generally negative about new initiatives, play the game differently. Be clear that in parts of the discussion you are inviting only positive thinking: ask people to talk about potential benefits and spin-offs, 'parking' worries and concerns for the moment. Later, explicitly ask for the downside – the snags, what might go wrong. Teaching groups not to blur positive and negative thinking means you spend more time looking at what might work rather than being tripped up by the idea that it can't

## RECRUIT SOMEONE TO COVER YOUR BLIND SIDE

Your experience may reveal that you aren't always the quickest to pick up emotional colour. If your radar in this area is not great, stop giving yourself a hard time. We can develop it a little with age, but it's fairly hard wired. Blaming yourself for poor emotional intelligence is about as smart as beating yourself up for not being taller or smarter.

What smarter people do is to recruit people at the opposite end of the personality scale. So if you are really good at people, relationships and maintaining harmony, draw someone into the conversation who is good at allocating tasks, chasing work up, and not allowing people to say 'no'. If however you are not good at reading the room, find someone who is.

If you have difficult news to communicate to a team, for example, run that information past someone who will be good at anticipating how people are likely to react. 'How will people feel when I tell them this?' is the key question. Listen carefully – you may be surprised.

An equally good tactic is to ask someone in a meeting to be a second pair of eyes and ears in the room. While you focus on the agenda, get them to watch and listen. This isn't about Big Brother surveillance, but an honest acknowledgement of what you do well and where you need help decoding emotional responses. What matters of course is that you make the time to listen to feedback afterwards about how people were really responding.

## MARKET TESTING AND TEMPERATURE CHECKING

It's generally easier to read people one at a time. Pack mentality means that some people will speak and others will think. Some will disclose, others will play their cards close to their chest. Let's take the example of a meeting where you are going to announce a programme of change that is going to require people to rethink their roles. You could take the risk of announcing the news with a 'take it or leave it' approach. Confidentiality may not allow you to discuss things in advance, and inflexibility in the plans may tie your hands in terms of outcomes.

Market-test ideas before taking them to meetings where they might disturb or irritate. Discuss contentious topics with a range of individuals; don't just consult people who are 'on side'. Approach people who need time to reflect, and ask for their opinions before you go into the meeting. Spot likely opponents and flatter them by asking for their early feedback so they start to feel some sense of ownership. After a discussion, temperature check again within 48 hours of an announcement to see if people have got used to an idea.

### Putting it all together

Resilient behaviour isn't just about coping with what life throws at you. It's also about seeing what's coming down the path. When people find it difficult to handle the receiving end of tough behaviours and messages in the workplace it's sometimes because they didn't see the problem coming. Often this is a lack of emotional intelligence – an inability to decode the people issues that are never be explained in the staff handbook. When people find themselves under attack at work, they sometimes claim that they didn't see it coming. Others certainly did, those colleagues more attuned to the world of feelings, nuance and emotional micro-signals that's often so hard to decode.

The concepts behind emotional intelligence are widely discussed but not so often drawn upon outside the training room. We misread people every day, often failing to notice strong feelings we have triggered. Check in with people before critical meetings, pre-negotiating consensus and heading off opposition.

Heightened emotional intelligence is, essentially, the ability to decode people better. It helps you to understand how your words and actions impact on their performance, but also helps you select from your interpersonal toolkit in flexible response to other people. Sometimes wisdom will also show you what is impossible, or where you need help.

Slowing down any process where you're reacting to challenging information can allow space for honesty. Being more aware of feelings means we become more aware of how we pretend to use logic to justify staying inside our comfort zones.

# 41 Go with the grain

> *'If you don't feel it, flee from it. Go where you are celebrated, not merely tolerated.'* Paul F. Davis

> *'In order that people may be happy in their work, these three things are needed: They must be fit for it. They must not do too much of it. And they must have a sense of success in it.'* John Ruskin

> *'I have always argued that change becomes stressful and overwhelming only when you've lost any sense of the constancy of your life. You need firm ground to stand on. From there, you can deal with that change.'* Richard Nelson Bolles

> *'Organisms by their design are not made to adapt too far.'* Kevin Kelly

> *'Do what you love. Know your own bone; gnaw at it, bury it, unearth it, and gnaw it still.'* Henry David Thoreau

With advice coming at you from every direction you might feel under pressure to change and improve everything in your working life, constantly. However, sometimes resilient wisdom is about recognizing what works for you, and sticking with it.

The business phrase 'stick to your knitting' warns against product diversification – going too far outside the norm can get some organizations into difficulty. On the other hand, staying the same for ever can be a recipe for decline. So what's the answer?

There are clearly times when change is required because things are not working for you. Consider the other side: sticking at it. This may seem an unwise choice in a world which celebrates innovation and development, and yet there are some individuals who accept promotions or new jobs without really being ready to make the change. Sometimes they are flattered into something new, at other times there is distinct peer pressure to keep moving on and up. Taking on a more demanding role which is the next obvious stage of your learning curve (see Chapter 15) makes sense, but accepting a job which adds to your stress levels while diminishing work satisfaction? This is a common career story, and one that strips away resilience.

Doing something that 'comes easy' doesn't mean that you avoid being stretched. The greatest artists work in ways that feel natural, instinctive, and yet push them to the edge of their performance range.

Going with the grain means instinctively leaning towards tasks and projects which play to your strengths. Conversely, it means trying to avoid work where you are likely to under-perform because it doesn't match who you are. Often we need to be stretched way beyond our comfort zones – that's different. In this case we're talking about that negative combination of tasks you perform indifferently and without pleasure.

Beware of change that is about someone else's agenda. Sometimes the next challenge simply takes you in the wrong direction, and staying with (or moving back to) the things you do best can increase the chances of sustained, assured performance.

## WORK OUT WHAT FLOATS YOUR BOAT

You don't need 100% job satisfaction. Aim for about 70% overlap between what you want to get out of life and what an employer wants to get out of you – that's normally enough to put a spring in your step on a Monday morning.

Some questions to help you identify the main elements in your mix:

1. Be sure which problem you are trying to fix. If you're unhappy at work, is your dissatisfaction mainly about your role, your team, your boss, the organization, or the sector?
2. Which parts of your job help you learn and grow? How much has your job changed in the last 12 months?
3. Look back at the factors which made previous roles enjoyable (e.g. independence, variety, creativity, learning, sense of purpose).
4. Of all the jobs you have ever held, what was the most enjoyable, and why?
5. Think about a day at work that left you with a real 'buzz'. Write down what you were doing, what you enjoyed and what you achieved on that day.
6. What skills do you exercise well AND enjoy using?
7. What are your personal values, and how well are they expressed in the work you do?
8. What kind of people do you like to be around?
9. What kind of work feels valuable to you and feels worth doing? Why?
10. What kind of work environment makes you feel more resilient?

## STRIKE THE RIGHT WORK DEAL

You might think that being valued requires a supportive environment. That's half true, but it's also about the choices you make, including being aware of what motivates you (see above).

We talk about being 'happy' in work and then back away from the idea because it seems 'unrealistic' – many feel obliged to choose between work satisfaction and a decent salary. Yet you will meet people who say they love their work, and some of them are very well paid. Finding a better overlap is about finding the right deal.

Once you know the right mix for you, you can start to compromise sensibly. You can only do this (1) when you understand yourself better, and (2) by learning to decode what is on offer. This 'decoding' is about getting under the skin of organizational language so you really understand what an organization needs, and how it defines success. That means good investigation – finding out about a job before you take it, and asking even more questions about the organization once you're in a role. This usually involves tracking down people who can give you inside information into decision-making processes, trends, and the difference between hard work and visible contribution (see Chapter 43).

## SPOT OPPORTUNITIES WHERE YOU'RE REALLY VALUED

In any working life things come along – the chance to enlarge your role, take a transfer or secondment, apply for a promotion, or test the market. Sometimes it's a door you push on, sometimes it's opened for you.

Recognize that there is always a degree of flattery and over-selling in every recruitment process. If the headhunter calls, it's easy to be seduced into a role which is a poor match, and the glamorous promotion on offer may mean bigger headaches and more paperwork.

Assuming that you can do the job well enough, there are four varieties of work/personality fit:

1. You don't feel comfortable. People are generally very different to you and find you a bit of an enigma. Your receive odd or negative comments.
2. You're tolerated. People recognize your work contribution, but you don't entirely fit in.
3. You fit. Colleagues like your contribution and your style.
4. You're valued – for your weaknesses as well as your strengths. You receive feedback which affirms what your employer saw in you when you were hired.

It doesn't take a psychology degree to see there's a link between the above scale and your levels of resilience. The surprise may be that you have more influence than you think in shaping or finding a role that moves you closer to number 4, simply by understanding yourself better, learning to talk about what you're aiming at, and decoding jobs and organizations.

## Putting it all together

For some, work is a frustratingly poor match for what they do best, yet they struggle to discover what they need and how to find it.

Knowing what you need isn't about fantasy or selfishness; it's knowing how to get best value out of your abilities. So much of our personal energy and self-esteem is wrapped up in work, we might as well do something that motivates us. In addition, securing or negotiating purposeful work increases resilience.

Going with the grain sounds so obvious it's easily ignored. It means essentially, doing what fits you. Understanding the right mix is relatively straightforward, yet often seems a mystery to a nation where at least half the workforce is unhappy with their occupational activity. Work occupies a big slice of our waking energy, so it makes sense to understand what is most likely to suit you.

For some this means work that is a natural fit. Fashion designer Ozwald Boateng was interviewed on BBC Radio 4 in March 2012. He mentioned that his father had given him some career advice: 'if something comes easy to you, stick at it'. So Boateng did exactly that, switching from a course in computer studies to fashion. His father said that this wasn't what he had in mind, but Boateng stuck at it and has built a highly successful business with an international reputation. Your talents are not always evident until you discover them, but if you discover something that 'comes easy', it's often a great place to start.

# 42 Watch out for catastrophic thinking

> 'When sorrows come, they come not single spies
> But in battalions.' William Shakespeare, Hamlet

> 'The sun shines and warms and lights us and we have no
> curiosity to know why this is so; but we ask the reason of all
> evil, of pain, and hunger, and mosquitoes and silly people.'
> Ralph Waldo Emerson

> '"It's snowing still", said Eeyore gloomily. "So it is." "And
> freezing." "Is it?" "Yes", said Eeyore. "However", he said,
> brightening up a little, "we haven't had an earthquake lately".'
> A. A. Milne

> 'We find things where we look for them, which is why I never
> look for a golf ball out of bounds.' Robert Brault

> 'If some great catastrophe is not announced every morning, we
> feel a certain void. Nothing in the paper today, we sigh.'
> Lord Acton

Chicken Little (also known as Henny Penny) is a fable with
parallels in ancient manuscripts. An acorn falls on the chicken's
head, and she tells everyone 'the sky is falling!'. The name Chicken
Little has been applied for centuries to people who exaggerate
small signs to predict calamity, especially without justification.

The term 'Chicken Little Syndrome' has used widely since the
1950s, described as 'inferring catastrophic conclusions possibly
resulting in paralysis and as 'a sense of despair or passivity which

blocks the audience from actions'. Drawing on the original fable, one of many from around the world which predict terrible outcomes from almost zero evidence, the syndrome is firmly linked to the idea that these predictions are not just felt but are broadcast widely, believed, and acted upon. The term has become politicized; for example, it's used by those who refuse to believe in global warming to attack the views of environmentalists.

The fable picks up an interesting aspect of human nature – what psychologist Alfred Ellis called *awfulizing* – not just seeing the glass as half empty, but believing that the glass will be smashed. It becomes a knee-jerk reaction to any crisis. In the ever-popular TV comedy *Dad's Army,* Private Frazer always announced, in response to the mildest provocation, 'we're doomed'.

The brain is genetically programmed to make flash summaries of situations. We form first impressions of people quickly because primeval instincts tell us to decide if something coming towards us might be threat. Our 'fight or flight' system pushes blood supply to muscles instantaneously enabling us to do either. Those working for the emergency services will tell you that when adrenalin kicks in time seems to flow at a different speed, and judgements flow into actions in microseconds.

So, under pressure, it's a powerful feature of the human consciousness that we tend to jump to conclusions rather than walk quietly towards them. The brain that helped humanity survive predation forces us to quickly spot threats, which is perhaps why some of us catastrophize, making the enemy seem more dangerous than it is.

## DON'T VERBALIZE FEAR

One of the important aspects of the Chicken Little story is that she didn't just think the worst, she told everyone she met, and they told everyone they met. Rumour runs away with itself. In the age of social media a whisper can find a million ears in less time than it takes to boil a kettle.

Let's start with what you verbalize when you think in terms of catastrophe. Something is happening and you frame that event in words. We do it all the time: 'nice save!' or 'that goalkeeper was lucky' – an identical event interpreted in two completely contrasting ways. Listen carefully to what you put into words, even when you're just talking to yourself. Say something aloud, and it always feels more true, more solid, than just thinking it.

For example, imagine that you are a sales executive needing a big order so that you can settle your mortgage arrears. You go to a meeting and you fail to win the sale; for many reasons, most nothing to do with you. If your first words when you arrive home are 'I blew it!' this locks down not just today but the whole future. Your partner doesn't know what your contact book looks like or what possibilities you can pull out of the bag tomorrow. In the absence of positive information we invent dark possibilities.

Adopt the habit after setbacks of trying to say something positive first. Not ironically: 'at least I didn't fall over', but genuinely: 'right, my next move is …'. (See Chapter 3).

## LOOK FOR BEST-CASE POSSIBILITIES

Catastrophic thinking always needs to be tested. The first step is to identify that you have in fact selected a worst-case scenario. Next, consciously look for and investigate best-case possibilities. A great deal of this is about controlling fear, and just thinking. If you find your wallet is missing, you will generally check all the places you might have left it before ringing the bank to cancel all your credit cards. Resiliency training developed by psychologist Martin Seligman for the US military encourages soldiers to address worries at a later time so they can focus on their present mission (see Chapter 10 on postponing worry).

Examine the facts of the situation carefully, and then adopt the habit of exploring the best-case scenario: not forever, not with blind optimism, but as a trained primary response. Requiring yourself to look at the best possible interpretation can sometimes take you quickly to the most likely scenario, simply because you're already applying optimistic thinking, and beginning to shape solutions as well as problems. Even if the problem does turn out to be big and ugly, you're approaching it from a basis of what can be fixed rather than how much it can hurt you.

# DON'T IGNORE REAL ISSUES

Accusing someone of Chicken Little Syndrome is a great way of trampling down critics, prophets and whistle-blowers. Pretending that well-reasoned predictions of system failure are mere panic-mongering puts your head deep in the sand and comforts everyone else who wants to do the same. We have gone through enough financial and ecological meltdowns in the last decade or so to recognize that when you smell burning there really may be a fire.

Just as human beings can turn molehills into mountains, we're also pretty good at pretending that major problems don't exist, or believing they will go away. In 2008 Dick Fuld, CEO of Lehman Brothers, firmly believed that what his investment bank was facing was another routine crisis that would be solved by US government funding. Fewer people believed that the Lehman Brothers bankruptcy on 15 September 2008 was the beginning of a huge international financial crisis.

In hindsight everyone sees how the dominoes were falling, but at the moment of crisis only a few people have the information or insight to tell us that the sky really is going to crash onto our heads. Listening to those voices properly, and attending to clear early warning signs which are facts rather than hunches is an important part of decision-making. If something big appears to be looming, don't ignore uncomfortable truth-telling.

## Putting it all together

Imagine you move into a new home. You don't know the area, so you ask the local newsagent: 'what are the neighbours like here?'. You're surprised at the reply: 'let's see. What were they like where you lived before?'. You think and then answer: 'friendly, helpful, good sorts on the whole'. The shopkeeper nods: 'then that's what you'll find here'. We find what we expect to find. If you find all your neighbours unpleasant, a change of venue probably won't change that. If you constantly expect disaster, that's what you predict, and that's what you announce when something goes wrong.

In war, or marketing, exaggeration has its advantages. If you make someone believe you are bigger and uglier than you really are you can win by intimidation. In terms of personal resilience, catastrophizing has real dangers. Accepting your initial perception that everything has failed, that the sky really is falling in, has nothing to do with facts and everything to do with sheer, unfocused panic.

Catastrophic thinking needs to be managed, not hidden away or suppressed. If your first reaction is catastrophic thinking, look at that carefully and try to see why it is a habit. Sometimes these persistent negative thoughts reveal to you that you have fixed beliefs which drive emotional reactions, and cause fear. The ultimate test is whether these responses are meaningful, accurate and useful, or whether they are just emotional 'noise'. Questioning and changing the underlying beliefs and values which drive them is an important first step.

# 43

## Focus your time on the things that matter

❝ *'Begin challenging your own assumptions. Your assumptions are your windows on the world. Scrub them off every once in awhile, or the light won't come in.'* Alan Alda

❝ *'When the urgent crowds out the important, people urgently accomplish nothing of value.'*

❝ *'When you have to make a choice and don't make it, that is in itself a choice.'* William James

❝ *'Any fool can carry on, but a wise man knows how to shorten sail in time.'* Joseph Conrad

❝ *'Knowledge speaks, but wisdom listens.'* Jimi Hendrix

One of the most frequent causes of work stress and dented resilience is overwork. Working long hours was once mainly required by workers who wanted to climb the career ladder or maximize their earnings, but in recent times heavy workloads have become the norm for a large part of the working population.

In a tight market few of us have much control over how long we work; overworking can be simply about keeping your head above water. Some people are doing jobs normally done by two people, others holding down more than one paid job or dealing with the uncertainty of zero-hours contracts.

If you include time spent checking communications outside hours, work takes up a huge slice of waking time. Work can easily consume most of your top-level energy. Overwork can be all-consuming.

Take an objective look at where your time is actually spent. Thousands of pounds are spent each year on time-management training, but the truth is simple: there are only so many hours in a day, and you can't dig yourself out of problems by pretending that you can create more time. If you accept the fact that your time is finite and your energy is not limitless, you might start to think about what it delivers. Let's say you're fully awake and properly energized for about 60 hours a week. Where does that time go? If you considered that time as an investment, what would the returns look like? What is your personal return on time invested?

Don't just work hard, work hard on the things that matter. These will rarely be about the temporary niggles and hassle of your individual job. Your job description is probably out of date, and almost certainly doesn't spell out how you might contribute to the big picture. That's for you to discover. Start by thinking about what topics are currently in focus at the highest level in your organization. Find a mentor who is senior and wise enough to decode the business for you, and learn the difference between activity and contribution.

## USE THE PARETO PRINCIPLE

It's a widely held belief that only 20% of your time is really productive, and that 80% of working activity doesn't achieve much. Whether the 80/20 ratio is precisely true for your situation doesn't matter; the point is that a large part of any working day is unproductive. This could be because you're distracted, avoiding work, or doing routine things that don't add any value.

Cast your mind back to the last three months of work. How much of your time was spent working at your best and delivering results that made a difference?

Effective time management is about protecting 'golden time' – the time when you are doing the 20% of things that contribute to 80% of your results. It's easy for that golden time to be stolen or eroded. Watch out for time thieves, distractions that absorb time and energy such as bureaucracy, office politics (see Chapter 28), chasing unachievable targets, collecting data that no one will ever review.

Getting caught up in trivia, unfulfilling work, and doing things that frankly don't matter is a common feature of working life for many; and if you're still doing these things when you're running your own business, frankly, what's the point of being self-employed?

Focus on working through the problems you can solve, not tinkering with the ones you can't. If that means protecting your thinking time, your planning time, or the time you spend motivating or getting feedback from your team, then protect that time with a vengeance. Explaining why you are doing this will encourage colleagues to protect their most productive time. Identify the skills you use in that 'golden' time to spot areas for future development.

## IMPRESS MORE, WORK LESS

Look for leverage. You have a finite amount of energy, so longer hours can only produce limited results. If you really want to work smarter, not harder, focus on the projects which make the biggest difference and have the biggest impact.

Look for quick wins: If you want to make a rapid impact in a new role, look for rapid results. Ask around: what gets in the way of productivity? What can be resolved obviously and cheaply.

Discover quick wins by undertaking a bit of trouble shooting. Ask your colleagues what factors, for them, get in the way of success. This can reveal obstacles, internal or external, which can sometimes be flattened with a little focused effort. However be careful when identifying improvements not to tread on other people's toes or to sound like you have all the answers. Offer solutions on an experimental basis ('this might help') rather than arriving charging in to the rescue.

Once you have spotted some quick wins, seek permission to implement a small handful of changes which are low on cost and high on imagination. But make sure you follow up on your promises or you won't ever get a straight answer about work problem again from your colleagues.

# TURN YOUR DIARY UPSIDE DOWN

Having examined your working week, try tipping the balance in the opposite direction.

If you have some freedom of action, turn your working week on its head to see if it helps your working style. For example, if most of your week is spent on paperwork, try spending more time with people. If most of your time is spent in committee meetings, try structuring a week when you work in small, action-oriented project teams. Find an excuse to visit colleagues or parts of your business you rarely see. If your day is normally full of meetings, try some thinking time. If these meetings are formal, try informal working groups with short agendas and a maximum 30-minute timescale (one organization limits meetings by taking away all chairs and having all the windows open).

Look at the effect of different working contexts on your personal energy. Do you find it easier to motivate yourself when alone, or with others? Look at your diary for the last two to three months and use a highlighter pen to mark up days when you felt energized. How could you spend more time feeling like that in your current role?

## Putting it all together

Poor focus on what time is for often leads to working longer hours with diminishing results, and ultimately to a state of exhaustion when you make mistakes and fail to see the difference between what's important and what isn't.

Getting better value out of your time is about researching and listening carefully, tuning in to the language of concern (what your organization is worried about) or the language of intention (where your business wants to go). Aligning what you do to these outcomes, even just a little, makes your contribution jump into focus, gets you noticed, and makes your hard work more effective.

Look carefully at projects and requests as they come your way. Sound positive without saying 'yes' to everything. Try to get involved in the projects that are central to your employer's agenda.

Watch out for diminishing returns. It's easy to kid yourself that your time is free and an endless resource. For the first 18 months in a job that will probably work, but there will come a point where pressure causes you to miss things and start to make mistakes.

Carry on down that line and you start to work even longer hours to patch up mistakes. When that time comes, take at least a long weekend off and remind yourself of why you got into this line of work, what makes you effective, and where to allocate your energy. If your reserves of energy and motivation aren't being met by your current employer, perhaps it's time to renegotiate your job?

# 44 Remember your values

You might by now have come to the conclusion that improving your resilience is about learning to develop a tough outer shell that protects you from life's hard knocks. Taking the approaches recommended in these pages will help you to prepare for hostile events. However the underlying problem with the idea of seeing resilience in terms of exterior toughness is that this ignores what's going on beneath the armour. Resilience builds from within. That simple statement isn't just a slogan, but an expression of an important truth which is that you will get more out of life, and weather more of its storms, if your inside matches your outside.

Some of this is about matching yourself to external circumstances (See Chapter 41); a great deal is about carefully matching yourself to tasks, people, and organizations that share your values.

We all take our values to work with us. Your values are expressed in work through tasks and outcomes you find meaningful. Sometimes this is on a macro scale: you're interested in what your company makes and how it contributes to the world. For others values are expressed in relationships at work and the way staff are treated. Ultimately, staff are more motivated by organizations and colleagues who share most of their values.

In his book *Zen And The Art Of Making* A Living (Penguin, 1999) Laurence Boldt discusses three different kinds of values. Universal values are the ones that unite us all: love, peace, joy, health, delight in the natural world, and so on. Literary classics remind us that there are certain timeless constants at the core of the human condition. Cultural values are the generally agreed social values of the day. They are the values held by the family, organization, profession, class and country you are living in and are expressed as manners, customs and ethical standards. Unlike universal values, cultural values change, sometimes very quickly. Individual values result from individual temperament and experience and are reflected in what we do, own and consume, and how we spend our time and attention.

## TEN STEPS TO IDENTIFYING YOUR WORK VALUES

Look at how values touch upon your working life:

1. How do you describe your values? What words are important to you? If you use words like 'honest', 'authentic' or 'quality', what is your benchmark for knowing that these have really been achieved?
2. What language is attractive to you when you hear other people talk about values?
3. What kinds of work seem more meaningful to you?
4. Look back at your work history. Where have you undertaken roles which felt like a poor match to your personal values? How did that influence you?
5. When have you worked in an organization which had very different values to your own? What did that do to your commitment?

6. Where have you worked for employers who shared your values and embodied them measurably? What difference did it make to the way you worked?
7. Where have you worked for organizations who didn't live up to their stated values? What happened?
8. When have you been asked to do things you really didn't believe in? What was the outcome?
9. How have you managed if you have ever been asked to act in direct opposition to your personal values? What impact did that have on your resilience?
10. How could you adapt your current role to make it match your personal values more closely?

## 3. MATCH YOURSELF TO THE WORK YOU DO

In his book *Drive: The Surprising Truth About What Motivates Us* (Canongate Books, 2011), Daniel Pink suggests that employers are still trying to work out what keeps people motivated in the long term. Pink reveals that three methods are likely to be effective, especially for those doing repetitive work. The first is autonomy (freedom of action: some people hate being micro-managed and prefer to manage their own workload). The second is mastery (you learn to perform tasks well), and the third is purpose (your work adds something to your colleague, team, organization, community or society at large).

You might feel you have little choice about whether your work is purposeful; you take what comes along. Balance that against the fact that there are plenty of people who dislike their work but don't know what alternatives might work better. Many don't really know how to find anything different.

Finally, consider what you already know – work satisfaction and resilience are strongly linked. If you dislike what you do most of the time it's far more likely that negative events will push your spirits down even further. Feeling engaged in work tasks that seem to make sense provides a natural buoyancy. Good work is often purposeful work. You recognize that a job feels worth doing because of a number of factors. Firstly, when you pack your work bag on a Sunday night you anticipate the week ahead with optimism and curiosity, rather than indifference. Secondly,

you find yourself talking about work as if it isn't work at all –
a privilege, a game, fun, a calling. This is work which strongly
matches your values.

## ACT ON YOUR VALUES

Look at the work you do from a new perspective. How much
of your time is spent doing things that seem purposeful: actions
that align with your personal values? You don't have to save
the planet every day at work – you might just provide quality,
courtesy, patience or honesty.

Working with resilient integrity can sometimes be about
monitoring how far your values are trashed. If your job is
telling lies at public meetings or making promises to customers
you know you can't deliver, that may start to eat away at
your protected self. It helps to have a friend or mentor to be
accountable to in these circumstances so they can help you see
how far you have crossed your own lines in the sand.

You might, equally, want to shape your contribution actively so
that it increasingly reflects the things you believe in. This might be
fairly counter-cultural behaviour (like taking the time to listen and
build relationships) or sacrificing profit for quality. People who
live out these values shape more than their own lives – they
can make a difference to those around them – small amounts of
integrity act like yeast in the mix.

### Putting it all together

People vary in the tasks they find meaningful, and our values
adjust as we change and age.

Values language is everywhere, which means that it has
become debased currency. Most organizations claim admirable
values, but whether they act on them is variable. However you
know when you're acting in opposition to your work values,
because these small actions eat away at you. Resilience is
frequently about matching what you believe with what you do.

Most work requires us to compromise. Again, the extent to which you do this is about where your values set boundaries on what you feel is acceptable behaviour. You may prefer only to release a project when you have checked quality at every level – but that may also mean that you deliver late and over cost. You may feel comfortable adopting a 'good enough' approach to delivery, but that can easily slide into doing things you can get away with.

Someone once said that managers know how to do things right, but leaders know the right things to do. What the 'right thing' might be is about values and context, and what it feels like to do work well. This might be about performing a task to the very best of your abilities, making something that will last, genuinely helping a customer, solving problems, or creating something that wasn't there before.

Integrity is often about doing more than simply adopting the values around you in the zeitgeist. It's about real awareness of how your time is, and could be, spent purposefully – in the fullest meaning of that word.

# 45 Get your life in balance

> 'There's no such thing as work-life balance. Everything worth fighting for unbalances your life.' Alain de Botton

> 'You can love your job, but your job will not love you back.' Cathie Black

> 'Balance is not better time management, but better boundary management. Balance means making choices and enjoying those choices.' Betsy Jacobson

> 'There's no such thing as work-life balance. There are work-life choices, and you make them, and they have consequences.' Jack Welch

> 'I've learned that you can't have everything and do everything at the same time.' Oprah Winfrey

Organizations have put the spotlight on life-work balance in the last two decades, partly in response to legislation on working hours, but also because employers need worker flexibility; 24/7 operations extend themselves to new parts of society every month. Behind frequent and bland statements about life-work balance is a hidden reality: it's common for people to work fairly standard hours but then to have to deal with work communications outside those hours. For example a senior manager in the banking sector may receive a call at 3 a.m. because a 24-hour call centre has hit technical problems. If you work with international partners you may find you are asked to join conference calls very early or late in the day.

The information age means that email traffic only slows down at night, but doesn't disappear. You may regularly find yourself checking your phone for messages before bed, and even sometimes in the middle of the night. This problem is exacerbated if you have a boss who tends to generate ideas and instructions in the middle of the night, or colleagues who use non-working hours to gossip or reflect on the working day by email or text.

Large numbers work unlogged working hours outside the workplace. Even workers whose organizations are focused solely on one country find that they are under increasing pressure to respond immediately to email requests, whether they arrive at 2 a.m., Sunday morning, or while you are on holiday.

Let's be realistic. In professional roles you can't switch your phone off at 5 p.m. every day and be completely out of contact. There are operational roles where you need to be contactable out of hours. However, you can set boundaries about the rules for contacting you (How big an emergency? Who decides? What happens if you can't be reached?). You also need to set your own boundaries for how often you check messages.

Having the toughness to resist everyday weathering requires good self-monitoring. One important area to monitor on is the balance between when you're working and when you're recharging your batteries.

## BEWARE OF 'JUST'

Tempted to check your email last thing at night or on a Sunday morning? Be careful of a dangerous four-letter word: 'just'. As in 'I'll just have a quick look at my emails'. Guilt might be a driver – you may believe (perhaps incorrectly) that your colleagues are doing so.

Often however we check voicemail and email out of hours because we believe it reduces work. We feel it's better to have early warning of problems. We like to deal with small tasks at the weekend or during the evening because there's one less thing to do in the morning.

Let's say a complex but non-urgent information request reaches you at 10.30 p.m. You might be tempted to reply immediately to show how committed and efficient you are. The problem is that by doing so you have moved the bar. If you answer once, you'll answer again. If you respond when something is simply important but not terribly urgent, you'll start to respond to routine requests out of hours.

Whenever you hear yourself say 'just' last thing at night, you need to hear what it really means: *I am 'just' opening the door to a range of problems which may ruin my whole weekend.* If you're on holiday and thinking you will 'just' deal with some simple emails to make life easier when you get back, what you need to hear and repeat to those around you is *I am now going to press a button that will make me forget I am on holiday and will fill my head with work problems.*

## BE HONEST ABOUT BEING 'IN DEMAND'

Go to any restaurant or bar during the working week and watch how many people are checking their phones for incoming messages. Some of it is about maintaining a social life or keeping up with social media. Much of it is watching out for work-related demands, gossip or problems.

Your phone rings while you are having supper with friends and it's a work call. Do you take it or not? Most of the time, you will take it, or at least listen to voicemail. Then you tell all your dinner companions, who are already irritated by the interruption, how busy and in demand you are. One manager I know spends every team meeting walking colleagues through his diary and constantly re-iterating how busy he is. He never asks about their workload.

Be honest about that phrase 'in demand'. Are your work colleagues really chasing you, or are you checking messages to reassure yourself that somebody wants you? A great deal of this process of checking in, every ten minutes or so, day or evening, during meetings, meals, while you are watching TV, is about reinforcing your own sense of importance. Being 'in demand' makes you feel a vital cog in the wheel, and while you complain outwardly, secretly it's a source of great pride, which is why obsessive checking in is habit-forming.

# MONITOR PROMISES, NOT TIME

You can't judge whether your life-work balance is correct or appropriate by counting hours. Taking an objective look at how you spend time is a great way of thinking about productivity and the real impact of your career (see Chapter 43), but a poor benchmark for judging how well you switch off after work. Even if you are home by 5.28 p.m., if your evening is spent feeling gloomy about work you have less energy for yourself and others than someone getting home at 8.00 p.m. tired but fulfilled.

A good benchmark for deciding whether your working life is in balance is to look back at all the unfulfilled promises you have made to your family over the last 12 months. Perhaps you said 'of course I will come and watch you on sports day' or 'we will celebrate our anniversary properly this year'. Look too at vague promises you don't really expect to fulfil such as 'we must get together some time' or 'let's have lunch when things are quieter'.

Resilience is strengthened by good social support networks. Measure your life-work balance by the promises you keep to the people who matter to you most.

### Putting it all together

One of the reasons traditional societies set aside one day a week as a non-working day is a very old idea that all things need to rest. This isn't simply about sleep, but about restoration and recovery. The saying 'all good work comes out of rest' contains a great truth. Do things when you're cross-eyed with tiredness and you won't be proud of the result – you'll end up re-doing the task, therefore using twice the time required.

If you know that you work better after a good sleep, organizing sleep is an important piece of work preparation (see Chapter 36). If you recognize that long weekends where you don't switch your phone on put a spring in your step on a Monday morning, act on that knowledge.

When you're not working, set yourself boundaries that help you to remember not to work. Wear a different watch when you're not working. Use a separate phone (or at least a different ringtone) for family and friends. Leave emergency landline numbers where you can be reached rather than taking your phone everywhere. Be clear about the kind of grounds you consider important enough to disturb you. Ask colleagues to cover calls and emails if you're on holiday. If you go into the office at the weekend, don't go in casual clothes.

Don't allow 'just' thinking to seduce you into peeking at work stuff, saying it makes life easier. It doesn't always – often it simply makes tomorrow's problem arrive sooner, and also signals your total availability.

# 46  Tackle change head-on

❝ *'The ignoramus crow of "love it or leave it" omits other viable options, such as staying and changing it.'* Bryant McGill

❝ *'No-one can persuade another to change. Each of us guards a gate of change that can only be opened from the inside. We cannot open the gate of another, either by argument or by emotional appeal.'* Marilyn Ferguson

❝ *'If you want to build a ship, don't drum up the men to gather wood, divide the work and give orders. Instead, teach them to yearn for the vast and endless sea.'* Antoine de Saint-Exupéry

❝ *'If you can't repair it, maybe it shouldn't be on board.'* Lin and Larry Pardey

❝ *'The best way out is always through.'* Robert Frost

The world of work is over-familiar with the cliché 'the only thing that is constant is change'. There are various reasons for the pace of change. Firstly, consider the impact of Moore's Law. This asserts that in broad terms technology doubles in power and halves in price every two years. System stress arises from the number of banks, for example, who are still struggling with computer systems 20-plus years old.

Secondly, stock markets are fired up by mergers and acquisitions, and organizations merge or adapt fast to avoid takeover. Thirdly, as markets fluctuate organizations find it difficult to predict the resources they need so offer less job security. Finally, change is a cultural norm. Organizations believe the best way to improve products, services and market positioning is to restructure and reinvent, frequently.

How people respond to change has a strong relationship to resilience. Workers typically feel their resilience is weakened when they experienced repeated change, particularly where they have had to apply for their own jobs. Many would suggest that three other factors come into play:

1. We tend to adjust more comfortably and rapidly to change which is well communicated and makes sense.
2. We commit to change more easily where we feel our views are recognized and we have some say in the way change happens.
3. Those who do best around change tend to be the most resilient – they are naturally positive about change, or choose to be so.

Look back at ways you have responded when change has been imposed on you: your response was almost certainly emotional, ranging from discomfort and irritation through to panic. New circumstances involve new threats to our personal sense of security, and it's interesting how these become magnified. For example, if you're asked to switch to a new computer system, your first response may be a feeling of complete incompetence. In these circumstances it's easy to verbalize doubt, and sometimes that can give the impression that you really are out of your depth, which isn't great for your reputation in a world which requires fast adjustment and quick learners.

## BE HONEST ABOUT THE WAY YOU REACT TO CHANGE

Learning curves (see Chapter 15) don't just reflect the speed you absorb information, they also measure your attitude to change. Some people thrive on change, others are slow adjusters. Change we initiate ourselves can be refreshing, but change exerted from outside can feel very threatening.

So, be honest with yourself about the way you respond to upheaval. If you know that you need time to adjust to a new idea, take that time. Coach yourself not to respond immediately. Take at least 48 hours before you answer questions about the way these changes will impact on you, especially if you know that your repeated pattern is that everything looks strange and difficult at first but within a month or so it all feels like a familiar routine.

If you know you respond better with support and clear instructions, that's what to ask for. However, be careful about what you verbalize – it's easy to project a stubborn lack of willingness to learn.

## PLAN FOR CHANGE

If you're responsible for initiating change, treat it like any other complex project. Break large goals into small tasks. Design implementation the way you'd plan any project. Look at the people and resources involved, and decide on your communication plan.

Be clear about timing, not just for delivery but also what needs to be done when. Build in review points so you can check progress. Be clear about responsibilities and how far people are enabled to make progress without checking back to the plan. Build in reporting points.

The same can also work to some extent for change that is imposed on you. You're bound to react badly to the idea of overwhelming change, but if you take the time to look at the details of how it will be staged that will allow you to slow down the process in your mind. Look at the proposed stages in exactly the same way you would if planning them yourself.

With any proposal for change there will always be flaws. Some of this is connected with unknown factors – variables you can't control or predict. Even the best plans have gaps, either because they rely on luck or co-operative spirit, or they will inevitably be altered by events as they unfold. Therefore it doesn't pay to constantly be the person who says, in varying terms, 'it won't work'.

# BE A CAUTIOUS ADVOCATE

Complaining about change in business life is as pointless as complaining about alterations in the weather – it's going to happen. Continuous improvement has become order of the day, and organizations feel compelled to change just to stand still. Accept that and you can see how important it is to plan ahead to tackle change head on.

Change has its unquestioning supporters and its hard-nosed opponents. Neither group deals with change well. The first says yes too soon, without asking critical questions. The second group adopts cynicism as a behavioural habit, and can easily slide into ignoring organizational demands in the belief that the rules of the game will have changed before you're called to account. That may be true, but you will already have sent out a message of non-compliance.

Watch and learn. Watch colleagues who make the strongest impression during times of restructuring. They don't broadcast unthinking obedience, but reasoned optimism. They ask questions about implementation and warn about problems, but in broad terms their attitude is *let's try it and see*. That may sound obvious, but those who carry this off best have learned how to do this repeatedly. It often feels like keeping plenty of optimism in reserve, anticipating that the current round of change cannot be the last (see also Chapter 2 on being experimental).

If you have to make a critical response to plans for change, offer your feedback in a positive wrapper. Start by talking about what you find exciting, mention your reservations, then conclude by voicing your commitment to making things work. Organizations have no shortage of negative voices; they need people who are constructively critical but still committed to the next stage of the journey.

Change can feel like a shipwreck, and it's easy to feel like a survivor clinging to the wreckage. Survivor mode often makes people look only at the short term: finding safe ground, escaping discomfort, getting out. It can make us feel negative about options available to us, and incapable of seeing the longer-term picture. Feeling like a survivor, just hanging on to a job by your fingertips and waiting for the next wave to hit you, isn't a great way to show how you can contribute.

Unchallenged, the survivor mindset encourages 'getting safe' thinking – keeping your head down, keeping out of the way of trouble, avoiding risk and commitment. This behaviour quickly puts you at risk of being a casualty in the next wave of restructuring.

We like to pretend that we have logical reasons for worrying about change: it will disrupt your work pattern, make it harder to undertake routine tasks, and will required a lot of extra effort. Of course *reasons* are your shorthand for *feelings* – uncertainty, doubt, fear of failure, worry that your job may be under threat.

Don't hide behind the smokescreen of personality. Yes, some people are naturally more responsive to change, even if this involves role discomfort. These individuals rarely need coaching around change: they spot opportunities to contribute quickly, and communicate enthusiasm. Your job is to work with *you* – bearing in mind that you have the power to decide how you will respond to change. Learn to be a cautious advocate, even where change is repeated and difficult.

# 47 Learn optimism

> 'The real man smiles in trouble, gathers strength from distress, and grows brave by reflection.' Thomas Paine

> 'Life can only be understood backwards; but it must be lived forwards.' Søren Kierkegaard

> 'In the long run the pessimist may be proved right, but the optimist has a better time on the trip.' Daniel L. Reardon

> 'If you deliberately set out to be less than you are capable, you'll be unhappy for the rest of your life.' Abraham Maslow

> 'Life is not about tenaciously holding on to and justifying what we have. It is about living as grateful people, aware that all that we are and have is a gift.' Marcus Borg

Psychologist Barbara Fredrickson originated the 'broaden-and-build' theory of positive emotions. She argued that negative emotions give us a narrow focus and push us towards urgent behaviours closely connected to survival (for example anxiety might trigger a fight-or-flight response). Positive emotions, however, do not have any immediate usefulness in terms of survival, and so with your mind taken off your immediate needs you see a wider perspective.

Positive emotions (such as happiness, joy, interest, and hopeful anticipation) are not only pleasurable but also broaden the way we think, allowing us to be more engaged with the world around us rather than focused on narrow concerns. For example, feeling joyful can spark a sense of playfulness, an interest in a subject draws out the urge to explore, and a feeling of contentment often prompts an urge to draw others closer.

The broaden-and-build theory describes the short-term effects of positive feelings on our attention, motivation, and even on physical responses such as a sense of feeling well. When you feel a strong sense of well-being, even for a moment, this fleeting experience can make you more optimistic. In addition, you open up — you become more welcoming to new ideas or expansive towards acquaintances, or perhaps you take an interest in a task which you previously considered uninteresting. If these positive moments happen frequently, you broaden into new areas of interest where you can develop valuable expertise.

This broadening of thinking does more, according to Fredrickson: it encourages impulses which move you towards innovation. It also encourages us to explore; over time this builds new skills and resources. For example, displaying curiosity about people you meet leads to supportive networks; while investigating new ideas can lead to the ability to apply them in practical terms.

Fredrickson writes: 'evidence for the undoing effect of positive emotions suggests that people might improve their psychological well-being, and perhaps also their physical health, by cultivating experiences of positive emotions at opportune moments to cope with negative emotions'. Broadening of perception this way helps us build skills, relationships, coping resources, and above all else, optimism.

## FIND A GOOD PLACE TO GO TO IN YOUR HEAD

One of the curious features of the brain is that imagination or memory, if attended to with sufficient concentration, can have almost the same effect as experience itself. Turning up an old photograph may trigger not just clear memories but associated feelings.

Some people instinctively know how to harness this power. Perhaps we all do in one sense when we say 'don't go there', meaning 'don't think about that'. What's implied is that it will be much more beneficial to think about something more pleasant.

This might lead you to distraction or escapism. You can however actively choose where to put your attention. Think of a time when you were at your best. This might be a work memory when you were really engaged by task, completing or starting an exciting project, or really on top of your game. It might equally be an experience from outside work where you felt a strong sense that all was well with the world, and with you.

Take a moment. Remember that experience as vividly as you can. If you have a prop to help, such as a memento or a photograph, use that to help you remember (tip: don't put these important pictures in view all the time or they will lose their impact). Allow the original feeling to re-play itself in you, body as well as brain. Revel in the warm glow until you feel a lot more optimistic about what you have to do next.

## ACT AS IF YOU WERE ADVISING SOMEONE ELSE

Change is often about adopting new habits, and about sustaining activity until you get where you need to be. If these activities take you outside your comfort zone it's easy to find excuses to stop.

For example, you may recognize that you need to build a better network of sector contacts in order to keep up with industry trends. You've committed to the idea with your mentor, and you know that building these new relationships are a vital career step which will allow you to bring new ideas into your organization and increase your visibility outside it.

So you begin, but after a good start – what? Perhaps after two weeks or so of enthusiastically reaching out, you start to flag. Now you are collecting excuses which allow you to stop: people don't return your calls, it's a bad time, it makes you look too pushy …

Imagine you were going to be paid to spend three months developing contacts for someone else. You'd set out a plan for opening doors, getting people to talk to you, persuading one person to bounce you on to another. You'd do things by the book but also learn which rules to break. You'd seek out information brokers to provide short cuts, and you'd keep great records, giving yourself targets and turning the task into a kind of game.

Doing things for for yourself you unconsciously look for break points – reasons to give up early. You get in the way of yourself. Imagine doing it for someone else, and do it that way.

## WRITE DOWN THE GOOD STUFF

Martin Seligman, renowned expert on positive psychology, wrote an August 2005 piece for *American Psychologist* about simple activities that increase well-being.

A group was asked to do one thing each evening for a week: 'write down three things that went well today, and what caused them to go well'. Seligman found that this simple task made a measurable improvement to happiness levels. In fact, impressively, this exercise increased happiness and decreased depressive symptoms for six months. The effect was even greater for those who continued the practice, but writing things down for just one week had an effect which was still measurable six months later.

A related exercise invited participants to 'write and then deliver a letter of gratitude in person to someone who had been especially kind to them but had never been properly thanked'. This, too, has a long-term effect on each person's sense of well being.

Two simple steps: write a proper 'thank you' when it's deserved, and remind yourself of just three things that have gone well today.

### Putting it all together

Positive experiences don't just delight, but broaden our responses and allow us to build long-term resilience. One important spin-off is optimism. Optimism comes naturally to some, others lack it, especially when the light at the end of the tunnel seems to have been switched off. The good news is that optimism isn't entirely dependent on circumstances or personality – we can learn to adopt it, at least some of the time.

Positive psychology reveals how important it is to celebrate life's best moments; by spending time with people you value, and by doing things that revive the spirits. The right kinds of experience help you think and feel differently.

Recognize, remember and revisit the experiences that make you feel good about life – not just as distractions or entertainment, but because such feelings make you open up much more to possibilities and drive optimism, which turns a chore into a learning event, a task into a worthwhile challenge.

When you have to do something challenging over an extended period, imagine how you would do it if you were passing the results on to someone else. You'll feel more accountable and realistic about succeeding.

Allow optimism to flourish: by getting others to help you find it, but also by rediscovering it from your past. You don't have to wait for life-affirming events to come along to rediscover optimism. Remember when you achieved something you didn't believe you could do. Remember five-star moments when you feel that the only way is downhill.

# (48) Toughen up

66 'A good half of the art of living is resilience.' Alain de Botton

66 'I think on some level, you do your best things when you're a little off-balance, a little scared. You've got to work from mystery, from wonder, from not knowing.' Willem Dafoe

66 'It does not take much strength to do things, but it requires a great deal of strength to decide what to do.' Elbert Hubbard

66 'Courage is the most important of all the virtues because without courage, you can't practise any other virtue consistently.' Maya Angelou

66 'In the depth of winter, I finally learned that within me there lay an invincible summer.' Albert Camus

Martin Seligman, writing in *Flourish* (Nicholas Brealey Publishing, 2011) argues that most psychotherapeutic drugs and treatments are about suppressing symptoms rather than achieving a cure: therapists 'dispense drugs or psychological interventions that make people less anxious, angry, or depressed'. Seligman argues that many of our response mechanisms are genetic: people may be largely pre-disposed to sadness or optimism. These strong genetic drivers can, in Seligman's terms, only be disguised or dampened down, not wholly eliminated. Seligman argues that positive psychology offers ways of maintaining well-being in the long term. Any 'cure' must be about a new state where 'the skills of flourishing – of having positive emotion, meaning, good work, and positive relationships – are something over and above the skills of minimising suffering'.

Seligman argues that we are locked into the idea that helping people move forwards is always about suppressing or removing negative emotions – the approach is palliative, like the drugs we take for depression. One strategy he proposes is dealing with emotions rather than suppressing them. He cites Winston Churchill and Abraham Lincoln as two famous depressives who managed sustained and purposeful work while having frequent 'black dog' moments.

This advice needs to be handled carefully because it can sound like it minimizes feelings of hopelessness, and can also sound as simplistic as the advice 'get a grip', however it does have some foundation in experience. We adopt different strategies for different situations, and in response to our personality type, but this one is older than most modern therapies – *just get on with stuff.*

In practical terms this has its merits, at least in the short term. In the longer term it is almost certainly wise to work out what presses your buttons and find the right insights and external support to help. In the short term this can easily make you an inert victim (see Chapter 6), paralysed by analysis. However as an immediate response, being determined to keep focused, keep productive, is an important decision – you remain in control and hang on to purposeful activity as your anchor.

# TRUST YOUR TOUGHNESS

In her book *Steel Angels* (SPCK Publishing, 2014), Magdalen Smith writes of the balance that ordained ministers seek between open vulnerability and resilient strength, and the fact that both require courage.

We often think of courage as something outside us we need to put on like armour. The experience of how ordinary people react in situations where they protect or save others shows us something different. For example when Drummer Lee Rigby was attacked in May 2013, two women whom the UK media dubbed the 'Angels of Woolwich' stepped forward. Gemini Donnelly-Martin and her mother Amanda Donnelly persuaded the attackers to let them comfort and pray with Rigby as he was dying. Gemini told the press: 'We did what anyone would do. We just wanted to take care of the man. It wasn't brave. Anyone would have done it. It had to be done'. Another woman, Cub Scout leader Ingrid Loyau-Kennett, asked the attackers to hand over their weapons, hoping to draw the killers' attention, later saying: 'better me than a child'.

The fact that ordinary people in a street in Woolwich can summon, untrained, such enormous courage is not just a moving testimony, but everyday evidence that people have inner resources they hardly imagine.

So, if you feel you can't face going into work this morning, sometimes the answer is just do it, and tough it out when you get there. What's the worst that can happen?

## SAY THE HARD THINGS

We spend such a great deal of time trying to find the right way to talk and listen, sometimes we focus too much on style and not enough on content: the most important things don't get said.

This can of course apply to things which are good to say and hear. We don't praise enough, and as Chapter 34 shows, thanking someone properly helps you as well as improving their day.

We don't always have the courage to say difficult things. What you say may come out as emotional noise ('I don't like the way I'm being treated in this job') rather than a clear statement ('I'd like to talk about the feedback I get for my work').

Saying hard things can sometimes be about speaking important truths. They may not come out measured, but the air gets cleared. You will find of course that they are spoken best when you have thought carefully, focused on things that can be resolved, and chosen your words with *some* care (don't let this be an absolute). Getting on sometimes requires telling things as you see them. Just be prepared to listen constructively to what comes back, not using any reply as an excuse to throw your toys out of the pram.

# DON'T GO THERE …

Consider people who make tough decisions and live with them, drawing on inner strengths at times of crisis. Ask them about the possible downside: 'what might go wrong?' These dark possibilities are what haunt most of us; the very thought of discomfort, embarrassment or loss puts the handbrake on. People who overcome negative thinking often just say to themselves *just don't go there*.

What might seem like putting your head in the sand is in fact an important feature of resilience. There are times when you refuse to let imagined futures overwhelm you. There are times when you choose, if you can, not to let memory fill your day with regret, sadness or anger. It's not 100% foolproof or sound, but it's still a useful mechanism – choose where you place your thinking, and don't go to the dark places.

Although this sounds like talking tough, it chimes with new thinking on positive psychology. The model we have all been using is about processing negative thoughts, working through them, emptying ourselves of them. New approaches championed by Martin Seligman and others suggest that you don't empty out, you fill – with positive pictures, memories, and plans.

You might also choose 'not to go there' when things are on the up; congratulating yourself too early when it looks like you might have a towering success on your hands. It's all about getting on with things and not being distracted by highs and lows.

### Putting it all together

Keep at it. In the words of the popular poster which hails from the Second World War (but was never used during it), 'Keep Calm And Carry On'. It's the foundation of the kind of resilience demonstrated in most societies throughout history. Bad things happen including starvation and persecution, but life must go on. Even in a city under siege, food is cooked, the sick are treated, children are educated. Without too much time thinking 'what's the point?', people just get on with things.

People doing tough jobs are often trained how to knuckle down to complete the task rather than learn coping skills. Trainee pilots learn the hard way how to respond during white-knuckle emergencies, not how to think about them. Workers who undertake roles that demand lack of sleep or prolonged attentiveness learn through training to do what they have to do with the resources available to them, focusing on getting the job done, not how things might be improved.

Working with negative emotions or under demanding external circumstances sometimes requires straightforward toughness. Not asking why it's happening to you, not demanding sleep, warmth or a clear head, but just doing the job. Moving beyond self-focused concern and a longing for improved conditions is what makes our strongest athletes and explorers, and sometimes what makes us good parents and citizens in times of trouble.

It's what has been called operating within your 'set range' – in other words, being the best person available to you right now.

# 49 Grab the steering wheel

> 'My life didn't please me, so I created my life.' Coco Chanel

> 'If you conquer yourself, then you conquer the world.'
> Paulo Coelho

> 'One can be the master of what one does, but never of what one feels.' Gustave Flaubert

> 'You can have anything you want if you want it badly enough. You can be anything you want to be, do anything you set out to accomplish if you hold to that desire with singleness of purpose.' Abraham Lincoln

> 'Twenty years from now you will be more disappointed by the things that you didn't do than by the ones you did do. So throw off the bowlines. Sail away from the safe harbour. Catch the trade winds in your sails. Explore. Dream. Discover.'
> H. Jackson Brown Jr.

Fifty years ago the working world was largely about obedience. The new organizations emerging in the 1950s in USA and Japan, drew heavily on those who had served, led, and organized during the Second World War, so it is no surprise that these multinationals adopted conformity, discipline and compliance as models. You were expected to do pretty much what you were told, including accepting overseas postings, and your learning and career stages were largely managed for you. In return, you received long-term job security, the social prestige of working for a major corporation, and a healthy benefits package.

The workplace of the twenty-first century is very different. Flat organizations have less management time available for developing and supporting workers, and reduced training budgets. Today's organization expects to reconfigure itself regularly, and its workforce to reinvent itself at the same time. Most HR Directors now have two major headaches – how to retain talent even though there are fewer promotion opportunities, and how to encourage workers to manage their own expectations, development, and career planning. Where these employers once valued people who took control of their own working destinies, now it's becoming mandatory. It's crept up on us rather quietly, but a great deal of responsibility has transferred to the individual.

This has major consequences in terms of resilience. If your work satisfaction and career trajectory is largely up to you, so is your happiness. This may sound simplistic, but the idea is important. We blame external factors – what other people have done to us or what life has thrown at us – but experience shows you that how you deal with experience is just as important as what comes along.

In some situations this will be about small steps - taking control of just a small part of your life. If you're facing multiple knock-backs in one year including redundancy, bereavement and illness, taking control may seem like a hopeless fantasy. Yet experience shows you that control even over the smallest things starts to help. You're making decisions, working around an internal locus of control (see Chapter 13).

## TAKE CHARGE OF ONE THING

It's easy to feel overwhelmed when problems come in thick and fast; often everything hits you at the same time. Even if they're single problems they may be complex with multiple causes and consequences. Although it's important to focus on facts (see Chapter 4) and to monitor the way you react under pressure (see Chapter 22), you put one brick back into your wall of resilience by taking just a little control of the situation.

For example, you negotiate to work from home one day a week. The request wasn't received warmly, and there is a clear suspicion that you will be less productive. On the second week of working from home a storm kicks in and you lose power. Your office is still connected, but at home you have no broadband and what's left of the limited battery life of your phone. A practical problem, but also an event that dents your confidence because you feel you are now even more at risk for asking for flexible working. This event will surely prove it was a bad idea.

How you frame events back at work matters, but less so than taking control of one thing immediately: using your battery power to complete one task, informing a key person of your difficulty, or taking your phone and a charger to a new location. One step forward sets a direction and encourages you to take the next.

## WORK TOWARDS YOUR A-LIST

Take time to remember highlight events experienced in work. Think about great days at work, your achievements, and what you learned. Remember projects you initiated and completed, and what felt good about them. You might think about five-star days from outside your working life. Holding these examples in your mind, write down what you were actually doing. Record the skills you were using, and the outcomes you achieved. Make a note of why the event was exciting, what it was about a task that kept you fully engaged (see also Chapter 41 on work drivers). This is your A-list: the skills, situations and outcomes that motivate you most. This list gives you a fairly clear idea of what the perfect job would look like, one where you would be more resilient simply because you were feeling upbeat all of the time.

The problem with thinking about a perfect job is that it pretends that job satisfaction is way beyond your reach. This counsel of perfection is a great distraction when it comes to taking control of your working life. You probably don't need much more than three days out of five to be pretty good – work which feels worth getting up for in the morning.

Move towards that goal quickly. Review your last 12 months of work: how much of the time were you doing things on your A-list? Where can you make a change?

## PITCH A NEW WORK DEAL

Once you have a fairly clear idea of your A-list, ask for a review with your boss. Make it clear that you want a discussion which is outside the normal framework of appraisals or performance reviews. This time you're offering an adjusted deal which is going to make work more interesting but also defend your resilience.

Talk to your boss (or the right decision-maker) first of all about what you have delivered in the last year, and then about what you would like to offer now. This will be a mix of good ideas for developing your role, and learning opportunities. The idea is to take proactive steps to make the job you do a closer match to your A-list. Remember that you are not aiming to get to 100%, certainly not in one step, but you are moving towards the goal of feeling you're in motivating work for three days out of five.

Pitch your suggestion as an offer, not a complaint. Your boss needs to hear how the organization benefits. If your ideas for role development offer some obvious wins, you should get a positive reception. If you don't get everything you want, focus on the things that make the biggest difference.

### Putting it all together

We talk about feeling 'swamped', as if you're in a boat with water lapping over the sides. In that situation, you do something: find a bucket and start baling, fix the hole in the boat, throw heavy items overboard. You look for one problem you can solve straight away.

Theories of problem solving often suggest you break a project down into small tasks which you deal with one at a time. However tackling something *immediately* means that you make one vital and powerful decision: you are not going to be hopeless or adrift. You're going to prove that to yourself by beginning with one thing, and fixing it.

Taking control is about moving fully into the driver's seat in a crisis and taking a firm grip on the controls. Apply this thinking to your working life as a whole. You spend so much of your life in work it makes sense to give yourself a balanced scorecard. Work out your personal motivation A-list, and actively match it against what an employer needs. Moving ever closer to positive work for three days out of five is a great way of keeping on top of your job and anticipating change.

Neither resilience or happiness can be bought, grabbed or imagined out of thin air. They require work, thinking, and more than a little determination. Most of all they require a repeated commitment to one decision – that you are going to take control of as much of your life as you can.

# 50 Bounce back and bounce right

GG *'Expectations are a form of first-class truth: If people believe it, it's true.'* Bill Gates

GG *'Life is ten percent what happens to you and ninety percent how you respond to it.'* Lou Holtz

GG *'Don't be afraid to take a big step when one is indicated. You can't cross a chasm in two small steps.'* David Lloyd George

GG *'The individual who says it is not possible should move out of the way of those doing it.'* Tricia Cunningham

GG *'Man's mind stretched to a new idea never goes back to its original dimensions.'* Oliver Wendell Holmes Jr.

The language of resilience draws on the physical sciences, reflecting the way objects can return their original shape and state. Bouncing back in terms of experience means getting back on track, resuming your former energy and confidence. Could there be anything else? There's a school of thought which suggests we can do more than simply return to what we were before.

The first level of resilience isn't about bouncing back at all, it's about acceptance of a changed state. We call it 'putting up with things'. Just getting on with things under difficult circumstances is a strong human characteristic: it allows families to bring up children under terrible political regimes and while enduring great economic hardship. The way we operate under circumstances is resistance and coping rather than bouncing back to a former state – 'just coping' can lead to long-term unhappiness or depression.

Basic bouncing back is about taking steps to get on track once again, or at least not to be seriously put off course by chaotic events. The assumption is that you get back to somewhere close to where you were before.

*Bouncing right* is different. It's about *fully* recovering from adversity. This may happen more often than we imagine. Bouncing right is close to what educationalist Dr Mary Steinhardt sees as the gold medal level of resilience; when 'you do whatever it takes to meet a challenge and in the process you advance to an even higher level of functioning and wellbeing'.

Bouncing right is more than just recovering any old sense of equilibrium. This isn't just recovery but restoration. It is not just about being OK, it's about being very OK: finding a new calm, a new sense of purpose. This is undoubtedly why some people are identified as being more resilient because of past trauma – what scientists call stress inoculation. *Nature* in October 2012, in the article 'Stress: The Roots of Resilience' by Virginia Hughes, reported that researchers believe that monkeys are more resilient later in life if they experience isolated stress events, such as a shock or a brief separation from their mothers, early in infancy.

## KNOW WHICH WAY YOUR COURAGE IS POINTING

Courage may be pointed inwards or outwards. You may need courage to deal with inner demons, to challenge the 2 a.m. voices (see Chapter 9). That's a courage which requires honesty and a lot of clarity so you can see the difference between reality and emotional fog. Alternatively you may seek courage to deal with external matters – people and situations where your influence and intervention are required. The most difficult of these are where you need to call someone to account, challenge a decision, or question the status quo. Plan such interventions with great care to make sure they are not just emotional outpourings, but conversations which have a reasonable chance of improving a situation.

Courage flows in different directions. Think about *courage to* and *courage from*. You may seek *courage to* help you move forward.

Taking the first step towards a conversation with someone helpful but intimidating, for example, requires *courage to*. You know you want to get there, and you're half-ready to move, but it takes the kind of final deep-breath moment you need before diving into icy water. *Courage from* is about mustering the inner resources it takes to move away from something, to move on to new pastures. Here equally stern questions are required. Are you moving on out of fear, or towards growth? Are you running away, or sprinting ahead? Are you putting behind something in a healthy way, shaking the dust off your sandals, or are you leaving something you should have mended?

## GIVE YOURSELF SOME GOOD NEWS

Remember how it felt to hear some really good news? Interestingly the news probably didn't have to be about you; you might simply have learned that something good happened for somebody you value.

Remember how it made you feel. A 'warm glow' is the usual expression. Everything else that happened within 30 minutes or so of you hearing that information is coloured with the same feeling. You don't just feel good about what you have learned, you feel good about pretty much everything.

Replicate that feeling if you can. Take some time to look back through your diary for the last six months or so. Imagine that each page has a temperature colour: cold blue for bad news days, warm red for good news days. Cast your mind back to a time when you sent or received a 'congratulations' card or email.

Remember the occasion? Take a moment to remember how that felt. Recall the overwhelming sense that everything was all right with the world. It doesn't matter whether that feeling lasted a second or an hour – recapture it. Don't worry if the feeling was in any way justified by facts; just revive it in your mind. Now turn your attention to your next task and see what a difference it makes.

Keep a page in your diary or a notebook to record good news moments. Drawing on them later helps on blue days.

## DEBRIEF, REMEMBER, STORE AWAY

If you get through difficult times, remember how you did it. If you kept a diary during that period of time you may have useful evidence, but most people record moments when they felt low and not what they did to get past them.

Natural resilience encourages people to simply get on with life. For some this can be an effective strategy – we know, for example, that about a third of people are largely untouched by traumatic events and can simply get on with their lives, largely unaffected.

Many of us need outside help as well as self-direction to cope with ordinary but troubling experiences such as bereavement. A road accident or being burgled can also throw emotional equilibrium out of the window. Undertaking something emotionally difficult at work is also far from rare, for example facing a disciplinary hearing, or having to tell colleagues that they are being made redundant.

In both professional and personal situations it's good practice to talk the situation through at the time, but also later when the incident is long past. Looking at how you responded to trauma and change, and how it changed you, is an important part of bouncing right.

### Putting it all together

We have looked at many aspects of resilience in this book – why it's necessary, why it's difficult, what gets in the way, and first steps to maintaining it.

Knowing the direction of travel seems to be important. Basic resilience is about getting by and putting up with things. Sometimes that's all we can do (if social, economic or health constraints set finite boundaries we can do little about). In some contexts it's enough – think of those people in our communities who consciously give up time and career prospects in order to care for other family members. Sometimes it's because acceptance of constraints in a good cause is the right, uncomfortable, thing to do. This we describe in terms of duty or vocation. People generally have more choice about how they get on with life than they care to admit – in the developed world we have an abundance of options and resources.

Behind all the studies into resilience undertaken today is one fundamentally optimistic insight. Whether we believe in the idea or not, and independent of our personality type or attitude, resilience is something we can adopt, shape, and grow. We can learn from ourselves and from others. Yes, what doesn't kill you really can make you stronger.

The good news is that bouncing back can, with commitment, imagination and support, be not just recovery of your former shape, but growth into a new one.

So here's to *bouncing right* – not just restoration, but a new beginning.

# FURTHER READING

Albert Bandura, *Self Efficacy: The Exercise of Control*, Worth Publishers, 1997.

George Bonanno, *The Other Side of Sadness: What the New Science of Bereavement Tells Us About Life After Loss*, Basic Books, 2010.

Laurence Boldt, *Zen And The Art Of Making A Living*, Penguin, 2009.

Alain de Botton, *The Pleasures and Sorrows of Work*, Penguin, 2010.

Robert Brooks & Sam Goldstein, *The Power Of Resilience: Achieving Balance, Confidence, and Personal Strength in Your Life*, McGraw-Hill, 2004.

Frederick Buechner, *Wishful Thinking: A Seeker's ABC*, Harper Collins, 1993.

John T. Cacioppo & William Patrick, *Loneliness: Human Nature and the Need for Social Connection*, W. W. Norton & Company 2009.

Jack Foster and Larry Corby, *How to Get Ideas*, Berrett-Koehler, 2003.

Barbara Fredrickson, *Positivity: Groundbreaking Research To Release Your Inner Optimist And Thrive*, Oneworld Publications, 2011.

Daniel Goleman, *Working With Emotional Intelligence*, Bloomsbury, 1999.

Mark Katz, *On Playing a Poor Hand Well: Insights from the Lives of Those Who Have Overcome Childhood Risks and Adversities*, Norton Professional Books, 1997.

John Lees, *Take Control of Your Career*, McGraw-Hill Professional, 2006.

Jean-François Manzoni & Jean-Louis Barsoux. *The Set-Up-To-Fail Syndrome – How Good Managers Cause Great People to Fail*, Harvard Business School Press, 2002.

Anthony Mottola, *The Spiritual Exercises of St. Ignatius*, Image Books, 1964.

Daniel Pink, *Drive: The Surprising Truth About What Motivates Us*, Canongate Books, 2011.

Martin Seligman, *Authentic Happiness: Using the New Positive Psychology to Realise Your Potential for Lasting Fulfilment*, Nicholas Brealey Publishing, 2003.

Martin Seligman, *Flourish: A New Understanding of Happiness and Well-Being – and How To Achieve Them*, Nicholas Brealey Publishing, 2011.

Al Siebert, *The Resiliency Advantage*, Berrett-Koehler, 2005.

Magdalen Smith, *Steel Angels: The Personal Qualities of a Priest*, SPCK Publishing, 2014.

Richard Wiseman, *59 Seconds: Think A Little, Change A Lot*, Pan Macmillan, 2009.

Andrew Zolli & Ann Marie Healy, *Resilience: Why Things Bounce Back*, Business Plus, 2012.

## Relevant websites

Advice on worry: www.anxietyculture.com

Stanford University's Persuasive Technology lab: www.tinyhabits.com

National wellbeing data: www.ons.gov.uk/ons/rel/wellbeing/measuring-national-well-being/personal-well-being-across-the-uk--2012-13/index.html

www.stress.org

Martin Seligman: www.authentichappiness.sas.upenn.edu/Default.aspx

Dr Mary Steinhardt: www.utexas.edu/education/resilience/about.html

Al Siebert: www.resiliencycenter.com

Daniel Goleman: www.danielgoleman.info/topics/emotional-intelligence/

Hans Selye on stress: http://www.stress.org/about/hans-selye-birth-of-stress/

# ABOUT THE AUTHOR

John Lees is one of the UK's best-known career strategists. He has written about the world of work in titles across the media including the *Times, The Guardian, Psychologies* and *People Management* plus a weekly column on careers and work for *Metro*. He has written nine careers titles including the bestselling *How To Get A Job You'll Love* (McGraw-Hill, 2012). His work and case studies have been profiled in *Coaching at Work* and *The Sunday Times* and featured on BBC 2's *Working Lunch*, Channel 4's *Dispatches,* and on ITV's *Tonight* – 'How To Get A Job'. He is a regular blog contributor to *Harvard Business Review* online and in 2012 wrote the introduction to the HBR *Guide to Getting the Right Job*.

A graduate of the universities of Cambridge, London and Liverpool, John is a Fellow of the CIPD, an Honorary Fellow of the Institute of Recruitment Professionals, was a founding Board Director of the Career Development Institute and the former Chief Executive of the Institute of Employment Consultants.

He has worked with a wide range of organizations on career-management issues, including British Gas Commercial, The British Council, CIPD, Fairplace, Harrods, Hiscox, The House of Commons, Imperial College, The Association of MBAs, Lloyds Banking Group, Marks & Spencer, NAPP Pharmaceutical, Oakridge, Tribal, and business schools across the UK. He has given talks or workshops in the USA, South Africa, Australia, New Zealand and Switzerland.

Alongside his working life John serves as an ordained Anglican priest in the Diocese of Chester. He is married to the poet and children's writer Jan Dean. They divide their time between Cheshire and East Devon, with occasional visits from their two adult sons.

# ACKNOWLEDGEMENTS

My enormous thanks go to all those people who have inspired or contributed ideas that appear in this book: Steven Benson, Richard Nelson Bolles, Gill Best, Julian Childs, Trevor Gilbert, Kate Howlett, Rosemary McLean, Andrew O'Hanlon, Carole Pemberton, Stuart Robertson, Sophie Rowan, Ruth Winden, Ian Webb and Julia Yates. The project couldn't have been completed without the wise advice of Gill Best, Valerie Rowles and Magdalen Smith who asked good questions about a range of draft material.

I'm also grateful to everyone who allowed me to road-test material in articles or workshops: Amy Gallo, Sarah Green and Tim Sullivan of HBR Online; Judith Armatage, Catherine Brooks, Alan Brown, Linda Byrne, Lindsay Comalie, Laura DeCarlo, Brigit Egan, Jan Ellis, Matthias Feist, Steve Gorton, Steve Heneghan, David Herbert, Deborah Hockham, Marcia Hoynes, Stuart Lindenfield, Liz Hall, Stuart McIntosh, Gordon McFarland, Sandra Preston, Rob Nathan, Karen O'Donoghue, Phil Steele, Martin Stevens, Janie Wilson, Robin Wood, Clare Withycombe.

I am enormously grateful to Victoria Roddam and Jamie Joseph at Hodder & Stoughton for their editorial support and good sense. Thanks also to my diligent agent James Wills at Watson, Little, and to my talented publicist Becky Charman.

Discover the secrets behind greatness

For more information visit:
www.secretsguides.com